TEACHING FROM THE TABERNACLE

TEACHING FROM THE TABERNACLE

C. SUMNER WEMP

MOODY PRESS

CHICAGO

© 1976 by
THE MOODY BIBLE INSTITUTE
OF CHICAGO

Third Printing, 1978

Library of Congress Cataloging in Publication Data

Wemp, C   Sumner.
  Teaching from the tabernacle.
  1. Tabernacle—Meditations. I. Title.
BM654.W43   296.6'5   76-3794
ISBN 0-8024-8563-4

Printed in the United States of America

To
Charles C. Ryrie,
my dear friend,
without whose constant
challenge and exhortation
this volume might not have
become a reality.

Contents

FOREWORD

There are many books about the tabernacle in the wilderness. A number of outstanding theologians have penned profound treatments of this important part of Scripture. However, this one is different. This book is written for the everyday Christian in the marketplace. It was not written to challenge the intellectual prowess of great Bible teachers and preachers. Rather, it was written to inspire and bless the hearts of average Christians who, from the pew, would like to take a walk through this exciting edifice.

This book is much like C. Sumner Wemp himself. Dr. Wemp long ago dedicated his life to the blessing and helping of people. The students at Liberty Baptist College, Thomas Road Bible Institute, and Liberty Baptist Theological Seminary know what I am talking about. He is vice-president of our college and the spiritual life director for each of our schools. His ministry in chapel, counseling hundreds of young people each year, and the overall involvement of his life in the affairs of others is proof positive of his love for people.

People with little Bible education will be able to read it with great blessings. Sunday school students will gain much from this clear presentation of the truths of the tabernacle. Beyond that, it is an informative book for pastors, teachers, and Christian workers to study. It is well outlined as an aid for good preaching.

This book is in the language of the people; it is easily understandable. Sumner is not attempting to "feed giraffes" but is heeding the Lord's admonition to "feed my sheep."

I had long hoped that someone capable of this kind of book would take the time to write it and make it available to the Christian public. May God use this book to the blessing of many Christians and to the salvation of many precious souls.

JERRY FALWELL

PREFACE

Have you ever heard a series of sermons preached on the tabernacle? If you're a pastor, have you ever preached on each article of the tabernacle? Usually I find only 1 or 2 percent of a congregation has ever heard such a series of sermons from the pulpit!

Why is this? Anyone who has made a careful study of the tabernacle will tell you it is one of the most interesting and instructional studies one can ever make. After spending a week in the Dallas Theological Seminary Library reading every book there on the tabernacle and every commentary on Exodus, I believe I found why it is preached so seldom. Books have not been written to make the material really preachable. There just are no sermon outlines available. The fact of the matter is, it is not easy to preach. I found it difficult until I really worked at outlining and sermonizing the material.

A second fact struck me, which is how fanciful some writers are in spiritualizing all the articles and going into such minute detailed explanation of every knop and bowl. The great debate concerning how many boards there were and precisely how the coverings were placed does not touch the significant truths to be expounded.

I have tried to make the material preachable and teachable. Also, I have tried to make it practical. The important thing is not to inform people with truth but to transform them with great truth. The tabernacle is filled with transforming truth. By God's grace I have tried to present these transforming truths simply and scripturally. May the dear Lord use these messages to the glory of His own dear Son.

▶ THE TABERNACLE ◀

A FIGURE   A SHADOW
HEB. 9:8,9 & 24   HEB. 10:1

EXAMPLES ∿ PATTERN
HEB. 8:5
I COR. 10:11

THE DOOR ~ EX. 26:36, 37
"I AM THE DOOR" JOHN 10:7 & 9

OUTER COURT
EX. 27:9-15 ~ REV. 19:8

COVERINGS & CURTAINS
EX. 26:1-14

THE GATE ~ EX. 27:16
"I AM THE WAY" JOHN 14:6
ACTS 4:12

BRAZEN ALTAR
OF BURNT OFFERING
EX. 27:1-8 ~ JOHN 1:29
EPH. 5:2 ~ HEB. 10:12

LAVER
EX. 30:18-21 ~ EX. 38:8
JOHN 15:3 JAM. 1:23,24

PILLARS

TABLE OF SHEWBREAD
EX. 25:23-30 ~ MATT. 12:3, 4

THE ARK OF THE COVENANT
EX. 25:10-22 ~ HEB. 9:4

BARS
EX. 26:26-29

BOARDS
EX. 26:15-26

INNER VAIL
EX. 26:31-33 ~ HEB. 10:20
MATT. 27:50, 51

GOLDEN CANDLESTICK
EX. 25:31-40 ~ HEB 9:2 ~ JN 1:9 ~ REV. 1:12-20

ALTAR OF INCENSE
EX. 30:1-10 ~ REV. 8:3,4
PSA. 141:2

EAST →

ASHER

ZEBULUN

JUDAH

ISSACHAR

DAN

NAPHTALI

SIMEON

REUBEN

GAD

MANASSEH

EPHRAIM

BENJAMIN

Holy Place

Holy of Holies

High 7½

30   75

150

15   30   15   15

1

The Teaching of the Tabernacle

Imagine a fifteen-by-forty-five-foot house, constructed of three tons of gold, five tons of silver, four tons of brass, and an assortment of jewels, fine wood, and fancy tapestries. This was the tabernacle, the portable house of worship built by a horde of escaped slaves. In the providence of God, the amazing project was financed by the farewell gifts to the children of Israel by their erstwhile captors, the Egyptians. Considering labor and the materials prescribed by God Himself, such a building could not be erected today for less than $10 million.

The unique structure and value of the tabernacle command our attention. Never before nor since has there been such a costly prefab structure, the epitome of simplicity to dismantle and to reassemble. According to the design of the Master Efficiency Expert, it could quickly be moved by 8,500 carriers when the cloud of His presence moved forward.

God devotes two chapters of His Word to the creation, but over forty chapters to the tabernacle. While He does not have to say something more than once for it to be true and important, His extra emphasis on the tabernacle marks it as vital to us. Hebrews 9:24 says the "holy places" of the tabernacle were figures of "heaven itself." This being true, the way a person approached the holy place in the tabernacle is the way a man comes to heaven! This is the central theme of this whole series of messages: "How to Get to Heaven."

Probably the greatest motivation for studying the taberna-

13

cle is that the New Testament cannot be fully understood apart from the truths it depicts. References to the offerings and sacrifices, the tabernacle and its furnishings, the priests and their service, cannot be comprehended without the background of the tabernacle. In it is contained almost every New Testament truth in type and picture, and each picture is worth a thousand words.

A quick tour of the building and grounds shows that this tabernacle, the dwelling place for God, had a fence around it which was five cubits, or seven and a half feet, high. (A cubit was 18 inches in length.) The fence, 75 feet wide by 150 feet long, had a gate or door facing east. This outer court, as it was called, is a picture of our earthly walk and relation to God. Just beyond the gate, within the fence, was a huge brass altar where the animals were sacrificed and burned. It is a picture of Calvary where Christ was offered for our sins. Next in line in the court was a brass laver filled with water for the priests to wash their hands and feet before entering the tabernacle to minister. This laver speaks of the believer confessing his sins and being cleansed from daily defilement.

The cleansed priest could enter the tabernacle, the place of worship. A rather small building, fifteen feet wide, forty-five feet long, and fifteen feet high, it was covered with unattractive badger skins, but it was exquisite inside. Its door, of the same materials as the fence gate, pictures Christ as the door. The building was divided into two rooms: the first, fifteen by thirty feet, and the second, a fifteen-foot cube. The first room was called the holy place. The Christian's position in Christ in the heavenlies is the parallel to this room. It was the place of daily fellowship and worship of the priest with the Lord. In it were three pieces of furniture. On the north side stood the table of shewbread, the priest's food. On the south side stood the candlesticks or lampstands for light. Next to the veil that divided the two rooms stood the altar of incense, which is a picture of prayer ascending as a sweet smell to God. A very thick, beautiful veil closed off the last room. This veil represented the flesh or body of Christ which hid the

14

glory of God from outward view and was torn in two at the death of Christ. This cube-sized final room was called the Holy of Holies, or holiest of all, and contained the Ark of the Covenant. Ark, of course, means chest. This chest contained the tables of stone or Ten Commandments. Aaron's rod that budded, and the pot of manna, as memorials. Above the Ark, between the two cherubim, was where God said He would dwell and meet with the high priest, Aaron. It is the picture of heaven itself, the dwelling place of God.

The tabernacle was portable. When the children of Israel moved, they carried the tabernacle with them, setting it up again when they camped. The people lived in tents according to tribes in specified areas surrounding the tabernacle.

Exodus 24:18 to the end of the book gives details and descriptions for making the tabernacle and for its ministry.

The Place of the Tabernacle

The *place* where Moses received his instructions for the tabernacle was "in the mount" (Ex 24:18). Mount Sinai was reached in the third month after leaving Egypt. The meaning of Sinai is uncertain; perhaps it means "thorny," from the Hebrew word *seneh*, because of its wilderness character. Moses received two directives on Mount Sinai: the Torah and the tabernacle. Law and grace. The Law showed why man by himself cannot come to God, while the tabernacle showed the way which man can come to God. On this mount God pictured the way to heaven, while on Mount Calvary, Christ purchased the way to heaven.

Some who do not believe that Christian things should be sensational or spectacular should consider Mount Sinai and Mount Calvary. When the Law was given,

> there were thunders and lightnings, and a thick cloud upon the mount, and the voice of the trumpet exceeding loud; so that all the people that was in the camp trembled. And Moses brought forth the people out of the camp to meet with God; and they stood at the nether part of the mount. And mount Sinai was altogether on a smoke, because the LORD descended

upon it in fire: and the smoke thereof ascended as the smoke of a furnace, and the whole mount quaked greatly. And when the voice of the trumpet sounded long, and became louder and louder, Moses spake, and God answered him by a voice (Ex. 19:16-19).

That was surely a spectacular scene, and it accomplished the purpose of attracting attention and fostering fear. On Mount Calvary when the Saviour died

there was darkness over the whole land . . . and, behold, the veil in the temple was rent in twain from the top to the bottom; and the earth did quake, and the rocks were rent; and the graves were opened; and many bodies of the saints which slept arose, and came out of the graves after his resurrection, and went into the holy city, and appeared unto many (Mt 27:45-53).

Just what they did or accomplished we are not told, but it would be an understatement to simply say it was sensational. God's servants need to get on the mount with the Lord today in order to see some spectacular sights by which to attract people's attention and put the fear of God in their hearts.

"Moses was in the mount forty days and forty nights" with God (Ex 24:18). While there, he fasted, feasted, and faced God. He fasted, for "he did neither eat bread, nor drink water" (34:28). This was a time to deny the flesh and all its appetites. Then Moses feasted on God's word; he listened to God's voice, for "the Lord talked with Moses . . . and the Lord spake unto Moses face to face, as a man speaketh unto his friend" (33:9-11). How great to hear God's word from heaven and then to share it with others.

Finally, Moses "faced" the Lord, but he could only see God's back and live (33:23). After Moses saw some of the glory of God, "the skin of his face shone; and they were afraid to come nigh him" (34:30).

Moses was alone with God. To be shut up alone with God would transform any life. Jacob found that out; alone with God, he wrestled with Him until He blessed him. What a tragedy that we spend so few hours with God. No wonder we see so little of His glory and know so little about His goodness.

How we preachers today need to get on the mountaintop with God, to receive a message from Him for His people, and then to deliver that message with all our hearts!

The Plan of the Tabernacle

The *plan* for getting the materials for the tabernacle is outlined in Exodus 25:1-7. "The LORD spake unto Moses" (v. 1). When God speaks, we had better listen, catching every word, getting all the details.

The people

Moses was instructed, "Speak unto the children of Israel, that they bring me an offering" (Ex 25:2). Here is God's plan for God's work: God's people are to bring an offering. God did not say, "Have a rummage sale, a bazaar, a cake bake, a supper, or use some other modern contrivance to raise money." Above all, He did not say, "Go to the world outside and beg them for money to build My house." Building the house of worship was to be financed by the two million Israelite slaves who had been redeemed from the bondage of Egypt. If we who have been delivered from sin's slavery by God's power are not willing to give to build God's house, who should?

The procedure

Every man was to give "willingly with his heart" (v. 2). God's desire has always been that man's devotion be not forced, but freely given from a willing heart. The response is always based on God's goodness to man. How tragic for the redeemed not to give willingly so that others might hear the Gospel and also come out of bondage! It has always been true that "every man according as he purposeth in his heart, so let him give; not grudgingly, or of necessity: for God loveth a cheerful giver" (2 Co 9:7). The motives of the heart, on which

17

God looks, make all the difference in His acceptance of our devotion.

Their offering was to be what they had in hand, from gold to goats' hair (Ex 25:3-7). What the Israelites had was by God's provision. God "had given the people favor in the sight of the Egyptians" so that the Egyptians gave them "articles of silver and articles of gold, and clothing" (Ex 12:35-36, NASB). All that we have today is by the grace of God, "for it is he that giveth thee power to get wealth" (Deu 8:18). When the Lord Jesus said, "Without me ye can do nothing" (Jn 15:5), He included getting our wealth, health, and all that we have. When God's people possess riches, it is because the Lord has need of them. He commands us to be good stewards.

In addition to the more costly gifts brought by the children of Israel were some humble offerings of goats' hair. Even the least prosperous person could have a part in giving.

The problem

Moses soon faced a unique problem: "The people bring much more than enough for the service of the work, which the LORD commanded to make (Ex 36:5)." If only we had this same problem in God's work today. Was such generosity due to fresh memories of the heavy bondage they had been delivered from? Did they give out of the depths of their love and gratitude? God help us not to leave our first love and forget what kind of persons we were before becoming Christ's.

"So the people were restrained from bringing. For the stuff they had was sufficient for all the work to make it, and too much" (vv. 6-7). Wouldn't such a restraint make a fine announcement for a Sunday morning church service? If only those who have been redeemed were good stewards today, there would be such abundant giving. We could build churches, schools, and mission projects for those who are crying out in need. Television's prime time could be bought and used to blanket the world with the Gospel.

The person

It is significant that in Exodus 25:2, God said, "Bring me an offering." We need to be reminded that we give to the Lord, not to the church or denomination, or to pay the preacher. Giving should be an act of worship to God, out of willing hearts, because we have been redeemed at such a glorious price.

The Purpose of the Tabernacle

The purpose of the tabernacle is defined in Exodus 25:8, "And let them make me a sanctuary; that I may dwell among them." It was to be a "sanctuary," a "place set apart" for God to dwell among them. For the first time, God was to have a house of worship. There had been altars such as Abraham had built, but no structure had been set apart for the worship of God. God had walked with Adam in the garden, had visited Abraham, and in the tabernacle would dwell with Israel. (In 2 Ch 7:16 we see Him dwelling in the Temple; in Col 2:9, in His Son; and in 1 Co 6:19-20, in the believer.)

The tabernacle had to be a portable structure, for Israel had not as yet reached their home in the new land. They were pilgrims in a foreign land. Today, we also have a portable place of worship: "For ye are the temple of the living God; as God hath said, I will dwell in them, and walk in them; and I will be their God, and they shall be my people" (2 Co 6:16). Like Israel, we also are not at "home" yet, but are "strangers and pilgrims" in a foreign land (1 Pe 2:11). May God feel at home in our bodies so that His glory may be seen in us!

Many believers would not think of desecrating the church building, but they will freely indulge in practices harmful to their own bodies, which are the temples of God, and think nothing of it. It is true that church buildings have been "set apart" for the worship of God and ought to be respected; but when we leave them, we do not leave the glory of God there in the sense that He abode in the tabernacle. We should be conscious of Christ in us (see Col 1:27) wherever we go.

"That I may dwell among them." What a purpose for the tabernacle! He did not come down to dwell among them because they were holy, but to make them holy. "And there I

19

will meet with thee, and I will commune with thee from above the mercy seat" (Ex 25:22). God's specifications for the tabernacle tell how and on what basis man can meet with God and commune with Him, and how God and man can dwell together both here and in the hereafter. This plan shows *the way to God.* How can I get to heaven? How can a man stand in God's presence? The answer is shown in picture form in the tabernacle. The finale is given in Revelation 21:3, "And I heard a great voice out of heaven saying, Behold, the tabernacle of God is with men, and he will dwell with them, and they shall be his people, and God himself shall be with them, and be their God."

The Pattern of the Tabernacle

The tabernacle *pattern* was given next: "According to all that I shew thee, after the pattern of the tabernacle, and the pattern of all the instruments thereof, even so shall ye make it" (Ex 25:9).

Hebrews 9:23-24 says,

> It was therefore necessary that the patterns of things in the heavens should be purified with these; but the heavenly things themselves with better sacrifices than these. For Christ is not entered into the holy places made with hands, which are the figures of the true; but into heaven itself, now to appear in the presence of God for us.

How can we come into God's presence? How can a sinner stand uncondemned before God? The tabernacle shows the way.

The answer is given in simple form in verse 23, when God tells us that this earthly tabernacle which was "the pattern of things in the heavens" was purified with the blood of "calves and goats" (v. 19) but "the heavenly things themselves with better sacrifices," even Christ's precious blood. The high priest went alone once every year into the holiest of all, into God's presence, which is the picture of heaven itself, but "not without blood" (Heb 9:7). The one absolute essential

20

that we must have to stand before God is not our church membership, baptism, confirmation, or good works. It is the blood of Christ. We must come to God "not without blood," for "without shedding of blood is no remission" (v. 22). By faith, be sure you apply Christ's blood to your own heart and life so that God sees it as the atonement for your sins. In the Old Testament a lamb was offered to God in payment for sin. Christ suffered and died for our sins, and you can stand before God, completely washed from all sin, if you claim Christ and His sacrifice for yourself.

2

The Decision at the Door

What is beyond that door? As a boy, I once almost joined a secret club. At the door to the initiating room, I heard screams and laughter beyond. I became frightened and retreated. Afterward I often wondered what I had missed, but I could never make up my mind to go through that door and pay the price to find out.

Israelites approaching the tabernacle first saw the seven-and-a-half-foot fence around it. They knew the tabernacle was the place to make things right with God, to worship Him, and to personally offer a sacrifice and have their sins forgiven; but to do so, they had to enter the door.

The tabernacle was enclosed by a white linen fence, five cubits, or seven and one half feet, high. Details for making and hanging the fence are given in Exodus 27:9-19. The material was to be fine twined white linen. Instructions were given that the south and north sides were to be 150 feet long. The curtains were to be hung from silver rods attached by silver hooks to twenty pillars or posts set in brass sockets on the ground. The east and west curtains were to be seventy-five feet long and to be hung from ten pillars. Even the details for the east gate or door were given. On each side of the gate, fifteen-cubit curtains were to be hung from three pillars. The twenty-cubit-long gate was to be suspended from four pillars.

The "fine twined linen" tabernacle fence typified or pictured holiness or righteousness. God is surrounded by holiness; as we approach Him we are confronted with His holiness and made aware of our lack of holiness. When Isaiah "saw...the Lord...high and lifted up" in all His holiness (Is 6:1), he realized his own uncleanness and that of the people. He cried, "Woe is me! For I am undone; because I am a man of unclean lips, and I dwell in the midst of a people of unclean lips: for mine eyes have seen the King, the LORD of hosts" (v. 5). Any man approaching God must see the Lord's holiness and his own unworthiness. Only then will he recognize the need to enter the one door into God's presence.

Description of the Door

What a magnificent gate awaited the Israelite's entrance! "And for the gate of the court shall be an hanging of twenty cubits, of blue, and purple, and scarlet, and fine twined linen, wrought with needlework: and their pillars shall be four, and their sockets four" (Ex 27:16). This beautiful gate into the tabernacle is of course a shadow of Christ, for He said of Himself, "I am the door: by me if any man enter in, he shall be saved" (Jn 10:9).

Colors in the Bible are always significant; even today they are quite symbolic and meaningful. This tabernacle door or gate was first of all described as blue, which speaks of Christ's heavenly character. Whatever one may think of Him, he must recognize that He is "God . . . manifest in the flesh" (1 Ti 3:16). It is not enough to say Jesus Christ was godly, or more godly than anyone else; He was very God of very God, as John 1:1, 3 makes clear: "In the beginning was the Word, and the Word was with God, and the Word was God. All things were made by him; and without him was not any thing made that was made." Furthermore, "And the Word was made flesh, and dwelt among us, (and we beheld his glory, the glory as of the only begotten of the Father,) full of grace and truth" (v. 14). In becoming flesh, Christ became a man; but He was a perfect man, without sin. This necessitated the supernatural conception and virgin birth. Unlike any other man, Jesus had no sin nature or taint of sin. Truly God and truly man, He is the only "mediator between God and men"

24

(1 Ti 2:5), thus becoming the door, the way to God. He said, "I am the way, the truth, and the life: no man cometh unto the Father, but by me" (Jn 14:6).

Purple was the second color used in making the door of the tabernacle. Purple still speaks of royalty. The Lord Jesus is royalty. He is first of all King of the Jews and the rightful Heir to the throne of David. His lineage as traced in the Gospel of Matthew goes back to David himself. He was "made of the seed of David according to the flesh" (Ro 1:3). But the Jews declared, "We will not have this man to reign over us" (Lk 19:14). They asked for the judgment they got: "His blood be on us, and on our children" (Mt 27:25). Oh, the terrible price they have paid for their rejection and foolish request! We can easily look back and ask, "How could they refuse such a King, who could have done so much for them?" But He is also King of kings and Lord of lords today! He wants to be Lord of the lives of all believers; it is just as foolish to refuse to let Him be King of our lives today.

The scarlet color represents the sacrificial suffering of the Saviour and the shedding of His blood for our sins. From the first shedding of an animal's blood in the Garden of Eden for Adam's and Eve's transgression, the offering of Abel, the altar of Noah, the blood on the doorposts in Egypt, the scarlet rope of Rahab, the thousands of sacrifices of Solomon's Temple, down to the last drop of the blood of Christ, God wants us to know, "It is the blood that maketh an atonement for the soul" (Lev 17:11). It is not enough to talk about the Lord Jesus Christ as the great Teacher, though He was that. If He had not suffered for our sins, He would not be the Saviour. We needed a Saviour who was willing to take our place in punishment, not just a good example to follow. People had the Law and knew the right way to live, but they failed to live that way. God wants us to know that the door, the way into heaven, is by way of the One who shed His blood to pay our sin debt.

In the fourth color, the white of the fine twined linen, we see Christ's righteousness. The white linen fence kept man out, for it was a reminder that, compared to God's righteousness, "all our righteousnesses are as filthy rags" (Is 64:6), and that man is bankrupt. Now Christ has come with perfect righteousness which He offers freely to all who will receive Him. God tells us that His righteousness is "unto all and upon all them that believe" (Ro 3:22) and do not need to try to establish our own worth. If I deposited a million dollars in the bank to your account, you would be a millionaire with all the rights and privileges of a millionaire. God deposits the righteousness of the Lord Jesus Christ to our account with all His rights and privileges when we believe on Christ as our Saviour. This is why He is the door, the way to God! What a glorious Saviour! He not only takes away our sins by paying the penalty and punishment, but He provides us with His own goodness to get us into heaven. He suffered on the cross as though He actually had committed our sins Himself. Then He gives us His righteousness and we have the right to go to heaven, as though we actually had the righteousness ourselves. No wonder God calls this "so great salvation" (Heb 2:3).

Dimensions of the Door

A look at the *dimensions* of the door reveals much. It was twenty cubits, or about thirty feet wide (Ex 27:16). The width of the door would surely give the assurance that it was wide enough to accommodate all who wanted to enter. Today we can witness with confidence: "And whosoever will, let him take of the water of life freely" (Rev 22:17). God is sovereign and has rightfully "chosen" some "before the foundation of the world" (Eph 1:4), but a right understanding of election will cause us to testify with the same fervor and passion as Paul and Peter, who wrote about election. Unfortunately some teach and preach the sovereignty so strongly that they seem to give the impression that they want to stop people from witnessing. Any teaching on God's sovereignty and election that takes away our love for the lost and hinders our everyday witnessing to them is certainly not in line with the

26

teaching and practice of the apostles in the book of Acts, and should be reexamined. The gate is *wide!* Our invitations should be wide enough to allow any and all sinners to enter. "The Lord is not . . . willing that any should perish" (2 Pe 3:9). Stop speculating about the elect, and start preaching and witnessing "to every creature" (Mk 16:15), as the Scriptures command.

Now, there is an interesting comparison to be made between this gate and the door into the tabernacle building or tent in Exodus 26:36. Both were made of the same materials and coloring, for both represent Christ. One was twenty by five cubits, while the other was ten by ten cubits, which amounts to the same number of square feet. The outer door was wide and all were invited in, but the door into the tent, the place for worship and service, was narrow. Only the priests were allowed to enter. One door affords entrance into "life," and the other offers entrance into "life . . . more abundantly" (Jn 10:10). Too many have entered only the first door and offered the sacrifice for sins for salvation. They need to enter also into a life of offering the sacrifice of self for service.

Demands of the Door

Hear the *demands* of the door. It said, "This is the way. Enter here!" No one dared climb over or crawl under. Jesus said that anyone who tries to enter heaven any other way than by *the door* is a "thief and a robber" (Jn 10:1).

God warns us that "there is a way which seemeth right unto a man, but the end thereof are the ways of death" (Pr 14:12). All ways other than the Lord Jesus lead to eternal death and separation from God. Some say the way to God is to live a good life, do the best you can, join a church, and be baptized or confirmed, but all these ways lead to death. A very foolish conclusion is that "we are all heading to the same place, we are just taking different roads." Why won't we believe God's Word that there is but one way? Jesus declared plainly, "I am *the* way [not one of many ways, but the *only* way to God], . . . no man cometh unto the Father, but by me" (Jn 14:6).

This gate must have been easily distinguished from the fence. It was easy to find, so anyone looking could have easily spotted it. No one will ever be able to say, "I wanted to be saved but God would not let me." The way is open to anyone who wants to enter. If he will come through the door, God says, "If any man will do his will, he shall know of the doctrine, whether it be of God, or whether I speak of myself" (Jn 7:17).

Many ask, "What about those who haven't heard the Gospel?" That's easy, "because that which may be known of God is manifest in them; for God hath shewed it unto them. For the invisible things of him from the creation of the world are *clearly* seen, being understood by the things that are made, even his eternal power and Godhead; so that they are without excuse" (Ro 1:19-20). Notice the plain, strong language of Scripture. God has made *manifest* unto them, has *shown* unto them; the things of God are *clearly seen*, they are *understood*. But the unbelievers have been foolish and changed the glory of God, which was manifest unto them, and made an image instead. If a child hasn't learned and accepted that two plus two equals four, you would never try to discuss algebra with him. Similarly, those who have rejected the ABC's of God will not hear the rest of the story! But if anyone accepts the ray of light God gives him, God says, "If any man will do his will, he shall know of the doctrine, whether it be of God, or whether I speak of myself" (Jn 7:17).

A beautiful example of this is in Acts 8:26-38. The Ethiopian from Africa had not yet heard the Gospel, but he did respond to the light which he had. Because he had responded and was ready for more light, God miraculously took Philip out of a revival meeting and sent him to the Ethiopian. When he heard the Gospel, he received it and was saved. God will see to it that missionaries get to anyone who wants the truth. Missionaries from all over the world can tell of just such incidents, that when they went into a new territory, perhaps only one person at first, but someone, had responded to the light they already had and immediately responded to the Gospel when it came. We can be sure that God is good and just; no one will ever go to hell who should not be there!

It took just one step to be inside that gate to the tabernacle. Today it takes but a single step of faith to receive the Lord Jesus Christ as your personal Saviour, but you must take that step yourself. No one can force it on you. If you want to get to heaven, just enter the door through Christ; He will take you all the way to heaven.

3

The Acceptance at the Altar

The odor of burning roast assailed us the minute we walked through the door. We had left it for too long and it was all burned up, gone to waste. My wife was heartbroken. It was such a beautiful roast and would have tasted so good.

Solomon killed and burned 22,000 oxen and 120,000 sheep when the Temple was finished. Probably millions of animals were sacrificed by Israel over the years. Why all this killing and burning of animals? Were they wasted? Could they have been better used to feed the poor? To some, such burning would be considered a waste, but it is not when we see it is God's plan whereby we are made acceptable to Him.

The minute an Israelite walked through the door of the tabernacle, he smelled burning roast beef. But what a difference! Nothing was wasted, for it was the sacrifice of the offering to God being made at the brazen altar.

The brazen altar was foursquare—seven and one half feet square, and four and one half feet high. It was made of acacia wood and covered with brass. At each corner, horns protruded from the top. In the middle, halfway up inside the altar, was a grate to hold the sacrifice. On the outside, rings were attached; staves or poles, also of acacia wood covered with brass, were inserted into the rings so that the altar could be carried by the priests.

The Prescription of the Altar

The first thing to meet the eye of one entering the courtyard gate of the tabernacle was the huge brass or copper

31

altar. Notice first of all that it was *prescribed* by God. In Exodus 27 is the record of the brazen altar, as it is commonly known. God said, "Thou shalt make an altar of shittim wood" (v. 1). The word "altar" comes from a Hebrew word meaning to slay or slaughter. On the brazen altar, all the animals were slain and sacrificed. This sacrifice pictures Calvary and the cross upon which the Lord Jesus was slain and sacrificed for us. Every time we read about the Israelites offering an animal sacrifice in the Old Testament we can remember that in some way it pictured the cross of Calvary.

It was an altar of shittim wood, or acacia wood, as it is more commonly known. This is a very enduring wood and foreshadows the humanity of Jesus, for He was to come as "a root out of a dry ground" (Is 53:2) and was called the "branch" (Zec 3:8; 6:12). He was "the man Christ Jesus" (1 Ti 2:5). The way He became a man is unique. Though He was God, He "made himself of no reputation, and took upon him the form of a servant, and was made in the likeness of men" (Phil 2:7). He voluntarily laid aside (or "emptied himself," as the Greek indicates) the outward visible manifestation of His godhead and became a man through the virgin birth.

There was a specific reason for His becoming a man, which is indicated in the last of Exodus 27:2b, where Moses was told, "Thou shalt overlay it with brass." Brass in Scripture always indicates judgment. When the Israelites had sinned (Num 21), God sent judgment upon them in the form of fiery serpents. The Israelites cried out because of the judgment, confessed their sin, and sent Moses to intercede for them before God. God gave a remedy: Moses must put a brazen serpent upon a pole; if they looked on the serpent, they would live. Sure enough, everyone who looked *did* live. John 3:14-15 clearly says that this serpent was a type of the Lord Jesus, for God says, "As Moses lifted up the serpent in the wilderness, even so must the Son of man be lifted up: that whosoever believeth in him should not perish, but have eternal life." How was all this to be? God illustrated by the picture of the brass serpent in the wilderness that Another would be judged for Israel's sin. When they looked at this brass serpent, they realized this substitution, and God forgave them on the basis that another paid the penalty for what they had done. The Lord Jesus Christ was lifted up for us on the cross as a sinless man, but He was covered over "with brass," or judged, for our sins. When we look at Calvary and the cross through faith in His Word, we understand that Another was judged for us and we are forgiven and receive eternal life.

The Prominence of the Altar

Not only was the altar prescribed by God; it was prominent. It was the first thing seen as one entered the door; he couldn't miss it. It was seven and a half feet square and four and a half feet high. Not knowing the precise size of two articles in the tabernacle (the sizes of the laver and the lampstand are not given), we cannot be sure, but it is possible that all the other furnishings could be put inside this brazen altar because it was so large.

In parallel to this in New Testament truth, God says that in Christ "dwelleth all the fulness of the Godhead bodily" (Col 2:9). What a blessed truth this is for us! When we receive the Lord Jesus as the sacrifice for our sins, in Him we are "blessed . . . with all spiritual blessings" (Eph 1:3). We only need to claim and possess them, even as Joshua was already given the land and was told, "Every place that the sole of your foot shall tread upon, that have I given unto you, as I said unto Moses" (Jos 1:3).

Every promise given to the believer in the New Testament is ours for the asking. We need only to claim it by faith to see it become operative in our lives, whether it be the fact of being "crucified with Christ" (Gal 2:20) and "dead indeed unto sin, but alive unto God" (Ro 6:11), or to be able to "do all things through Christ which strengtheneth me" (Phil 4:13). How tragic to see a child of God go around defeated and wasting a life that could be filled with God's glory and blessing, simply because he does not realize all that he has through Christ. The riches of the truth of what is ours "in Christ" (Eph 1:3), as recorded in the book of Ephesians alone, will thrill your soul.

The brazen altar was also prominent in that it was by far the most often used of all the tabernacle furniture. The high priest went into the Holy of Holies only once a year. He went into the holy place morning and evening, but he was at the altar all through the day as the people came with their sacrifices. This should be true in our preaching today. Paul was "determined not to know any thing among you, save Jesus Christ, and him crucified" (1 Co 2:2). In 1 Corinthians 1:11-25 great stress is put upon "preaching of the cross." Much that is called Gospel preaching today is a million miles from it, for not one word is mentioned about the cross or Christ's death for sinners. Occasionally a preacher has the audacity to stand and beg lost people to be saved when he has not told them a thing about how to be saved. If we leave the cross out of our witnessing, we have left out everything. There is no salvation apart from it.

In so many Gospel tracts today, there is not one word about Christ suffering for sins, but people are exhorted "to give their hearts to Christ" or "to ask Jesus to come into their heart." The Word of God clearly tells us to preach the Gospel, "how that Christ died for our sins . . . was buried, and . . . rose again" (1 Co 15:3) and exhort sinners to "believe" this Good News for themselves. Most preachers would vow and declare they "preach the Gospel" and give the Gospel in their witnessing, but one who listens carefully will discern how little is mentioned of the cross, whether in public, private, or print. As Vance Havner has said, "They almost say it, and most will think they have said it, but they make a neat detour at the cross."

The cross also ought to be prominent in our personal lives. As Paul says in Galatians 6:14, "God forbid that I should glory, save in the cross of our Lord Jesus Christ, by whom the world is crucified unto me, and I unto the world." The preaching of the cross is the dividing point among preachers and people today. It will keep our hearts warm toward the Lord Jesus. The more we "survey the wondrous cross," the more we will love Christ and the more our hearts will overflow with thankfulness for our salvation. Too often we forget what a great price was paid for us. And when we look to the cross, "the things of earth will grow strangely dim." How shallow and insignificant is all the world when compared to the Lord Jesus and what He has done for us. Then, too, as Galatians 6:14 indicates, we will see that we are "crucified unto . . . the world," and will love not this world nor the things that are in the world. Yes, the altar was very prominent in the tabernacle. Is it prominent in your life today?

The Presentation at the Altar

The altar was the place of personal presentation of sacrifice and public profession of faith. Some of the details for offering a sacrifice as a whole burnt offering are in Leviticus 1:2-5.

> Speak unto the children of Israel, and say unto them, If any man of you bring an offering unto the Lord, ye shall bring your offering of the cattle, even of the herd, and of the flock. If his offering be a burnt sacrifice of the herd, let him offer a male without blemish: he shall offer it of his own voluntary will at the door of the tabernacle of the congregation before the Lord. And he shall put his hand upon the head of the burnt offering; and it shall be accepted for him to make atonement for him. And he shall kill the bullock before the Lord: and the priests, Aaron's sons, shall bring the blood, and sprinkle the blood round about upon the altar that is by the door of the tabernacle of the congregation.

The offerer brought his offering personally and willingly. At the moment we are saved today, it must be just as real as if we reached out and extended a lamb in our hands to the Lord and that Lamb were the Lord Jesus, "the Lamb of God, which taketh away the sin of the world" (Jn 1:29). God looks at the offering we make just as He looked at the offering of Cain and Abel.

The sinner coming to the brazen altar was to put his hands upon the head of the animal, thus identifying the offering to be his. In the type of Christ as the scapegoat (Lev 16:21), they confessed their sins over the goat and, in type, laid their sins on the goat, and the animal bore them away. This was fulfilled when God "laid on him the iniquity of us all" (Is 53:6). Praise God, He said the offering "shall be accepted for him to make atonement for him" (Lev 1:4).

This offering was an open public profession or act. Today, too often when people make a public profession of faith in Christ, nothing is mentioned or thought of in connection with a personal acknowledgment of Christ as their sacrifice or Saviour from sin. They state too glibly that they believe in Christ, but often they simply mean they believe there was a person named Christ, and they know nothing about His atonement. Public profession should mean that we identify ourselves with Christ on the cross and say that He died for our sins, and therefore we believe we will go to heaven.

The Propitiation at the Altar

The altar was propitious. That is, the sacrifice made there was satisfying to God for man's sins. Exodus 27:2 mentions the horns of the altar, and horns in the Bible speak of power. We praise God that there is enough power to forgive the guiltiest and to cleanse the vilest sinner. The horns were used to hold the sacrifices: "Bind the sacrifice with cords, even unto the horns of the altar" (Ps 118:27). The Lord Jesus was bound with cords of love and nails of hate to the cross, for He said of His life, "No man taketh it from me, but I lay it down" (Jn 10:18).

A grate of a network of brass was made and put into "the midst" of the altar (Ex 27:4-5). This made it on the level with the Mercy Seat, where God had said, "I will meet with thee" (25:22). Once a year, on the Day of Atonement, the shed blood was brought into God's presence and sprinkled on the Mercy Seat. The word for Mercy Seat in Greek is the word for "propitiation." God tells us Christ "is the propitiation for our sins" (1 Jn 2:2). "Propitiation" means to be made satisfied. God is made satisfied when He sees the blood. Sin, then, is punished, justice is carried out, and God's holiness is propitiated, so that God can freely forgive us our sins.

The sacrifice was killed in plain view but burned in the pit halfway down inside the altar. When the Lord Jesus hung on the cross, it was in plain view; but when God "laid on him the iniquity of us all," darkness came over the earth so that no one saw Him suffering on the cross with our sins on Him from the sixth to the ninth hour (Mt 27:45-46). This was too sacred for sinful human eyes to behold. About the ninth hour the Lord Jesus cried, "My God, my God, why hast thou forsaken me?" (v. 46). The Lord Jesus "suffered for sins" (1 Pe 3:18) far more at the hand of God in being separated from Him than He did in physical agony caused by the nails of the cross. Have you ever realized that Christ not only died but suffered for you?

The altar was propitiatory because God Himself sent fire from heaven and consumed the first sacrifice made on the altar. Right after the priests were consecrated for the tabernacle service and the first sacrifice was laid on the altar, "there came a fire out from before the LORD, and consumed upon the altar the burnt offering and the fat: which when all the people saw, they shouted, and fell on their faces" (Lev 9:24). God showed His acceptance of the sacrifice and said, "The fire shall ever be burning upon the altar; it shall never go out" (Lev 6:13). Why never go out? Because the people never would stop sinning, and the sacrifice was made only as an IOU for past sins. It was not enough to make one offering for past sins and to think that sincerity or a good life from then on would take care of or cover sins committed after the sacrifice. They had to offer a sacrifice for those sins, too.

When we accept Christ today as our personal Saviour, we do not accept Him only for past sins; He died for *all* our sins, past, present, and future. If we were to trust Him only for past sins and feel our works would keep us saved, we would have to be punished for the sins committed after we are saved, "for

37

the wages of sin is death" (Ro 6:23), and nothing else will satisfy God.

Fire has always symbolized God's judgment from the fire of Sodom and Gomorrah until the final lake of fire for all eternity. We should be glad that the fire fell on the sacrifice on the brazen altar to show that God accepted it and that judgment need not fall on us. The altar is the place of acceptance. God, in accepting the sacrifice, showed that He would accept the sacrifice of Another in our place. Will we accept this sacrifice for our sins and by faith offer Him to God as our own Saviour? When we do, we are told that we are "accepted in the beloved" (Eph 1:6). None of us dare stand in our own righteousnesses when God tells us plainly that they are "filthy rags" (Is 64:6). Remember, it is Christ, not the Church; the Saviour, not the sacraments; the work of Christ, not the work of His creatures; grace, not grit; which will get us to heaven, that all the glory might be to *Him*.

4

The Washing at the Laver

The Definition of the Laver

"Laver" is the same word from which we get our word "lavatory." It simply means "a place for washing." The priests were commanded to wash here before entering the holy place (Ex 30:18-21). It is a picture of the believer being cleansed from the sins he commits after he is saved. While the brazen altar is associated with a person receiving Christ and becoming saved, the laver is associated with cleansing for the sins he commits after salvation. We know nothing about the size or shape of the laver, for no dimensions or directions are given for making it; the priests were just told to wash in it.

The laver was made from the brass "lookingglasses [polished brass mirrors] of the women . . . which assembled at the door of the tabernacle" (Ex 38:8). A very suggestive parallel is here. Pride makes us look into a mirror, for tremendous importance is put on one's appearance. We are all concerned about how we look to others. Millions of dollars are spent on hairdos, makeup, and fine clothes. This concern is not wrong in itself unless it violates God's command to be dressed in modest apparel outwardly, but godliness inwardly (1 Ti 2: 9-10). To give up their mirrors and not worry about outward looks represented real sacrifice to the Israelite women. It would be difficult for us. God is not saying we should go about unkempt, but that we should be much more concerned about spiritual cleanliness and beauty before the

Lord. "For bodily exercise profiteth little: but godliness is profitable unto all things," and "godliness with contentment is great gain. For we brought nothing into this world, and it is certain we can carry nothing out. And having food and raiment let us be therewith content" (1 Ti 4:8; 6:6-8).

If we gave up just a little of the time spent in washing and beautifying our skin, and spent that time washing and beautifying our souls, we could see lives transformed overnight.

The instructions for washing at the laver are in Exodus 30:17-21:

> And the LORD spake unto Moses, saying, Thou shalt also make a laver of brass, and his foot also of brass, to wash withal: and thou shalt put it between the tabernacle of the congregation and the altar, and thou shalt put water therein. For Aaron and his sons shall wash their hands and their feet thereat: when they go into the tabernacle of the congregation, they shall wash with water, that they die not; or when they come near to the altar to minister, to burn offering made by fire unto the LORD: so they shall wash their hands and their feet, that they die not: and it shall be a statute for ever to them, even to him and to his seed throughout their generations.

In this section we consider four outstanding factors: the people, the place, the purpose, and the procedure of the washing.

The People at the Laver

The people who were told to wash were the priests coming into the tabernacle to minister before the Lord (see Ex 30:18-21). Only the priests were allowed inside the holy place to worship before the Lord. The priests were born of the tribe of Levi and ordained by the Lord for the tabernacle service. God's Word declares that now all who are born of God are His priests. "But ye are a chosen generation, a royal priesthood, an holy nation, a peculiar people; that ye should shew forth the praises of him who hath called you out of darkness into his marvellous light" (1 Pe 2:9). We are also called a "kingdom, priests to His God" (Rev 1:6, NASB). What a glorious truth that each of us has the right to come before God! We are invited by God to come spiritually into the holy place for worship. Not just the select few can pray or worship before Him, but all who are born again into this royal "tribe" have the equal privilege to "come boldly unto the throne of grace" (Heb 4:16).

The Place of the Laver

The laver was "between the tabernacle of the congregation and the altar" (Ex 30:18). This was the next piece of furniture located beyond the brazen altar on the way into the holy place. Everything in the court, or the open area of the tabernacle enclosed by the fence, was made or covered with brass. Brass, speaking of judgment, is also the picture of our earthly experiences. One of the first things a believer needs to learn is what to do when he sins after he is saved. What are the consequences and the cure? The laver answers these queries. At the brazen altar we see Christ judged for our sins, which brings us into an eternal relationship with the Lord through salvation. At the brazen laver we judge ourselves for our daily sins, and this restores the fellowship with the Lord broken by those sins.

When we accept the Lord Jesus Christ as personal Saviour, we are born of God, with His kind of life, eternal life, and we will never perish (Jn 3:16; 5:24). When we sin after that, then it breaks our *fellowship* with the Lord but does not change our *relationship*. If my son does something wrong, he is still my son. He may not enjoy being my son when I spank him, but he is still my son by birth, and nothing can change that. So it is with God and His children. We are children of God by birth, a relationship far more permanent than earthly ties. It is everlasting, for nothing can "separate us from the love of God, which is in Christ Jesus our Lord" (Ro 8:39b). We are in the Father's hand and no one can pluck us out (Jn 10:28-29). If we claim to have been saved a while and then, because of

41

some sin, say we are no longer saved nor have eternal life, then we never were saved to begin with. Christ alone is the Author of "eternal salvation" (Heb 5:9). But what about that sin committed after we were saved? Christ has already suffered for that sin, too, or we would have to suffer for it in hell; nothing else could satisfy God's justice. "The wages of sin is *death*; but the gift of God is eternal life" (Ro 6:23).

Usually unbelievers accuse those who believe in eternal security—once saved always saved—of thinking they can be saved and then go out and live like the devil himself and still go to heaven. That is a very foolish and perverted idea of a wonderful truth. A parallel would be to say you can get married and then have the privilege of treating your spouse any way you want; that is, mistreat your spouse, commit adultery, and generally live wildly just because he vowed to be married "until death do us part"! A rather absurd idea, isn't it? No more absurd than the false implications and applications some make of the wonderful truth that, when a person is saved or born again, he will "never perish" (Jn 10:28).

First, someone who "says" he is saved and then lives like the devil himself is just proving he still is the devil's child. God's Word says, "They went out from us, but they were not of us; for if they had been of us, they would no doubt have continued with us: but they went out, that they might be made manifest that they were not all of us" (1 Jn 2:19). This perverted idea also fails to take into account that when one is born again or saved that "he is a new creature: old things are passed away; behold, all things are become new" (2 Co 5:17). He has a new nature (2 Pe 1:4) and won't want to live like the devil! Also, he now loves the Lord Jesus and certainly won't want to mistreat the Lord Jesus any more than he would want to mistreat his spouse!

The Purpose of the Laver

The *purpose* of the laver was for the priests to "wash their hands and their feet thereat" (Ex 30:19). The Christian life is referred to repeatedly as a "walk." Believers are told to "walk worthy of the vocation wherewith ye are called" (Eph 4:1); "walk as children of light" (5:8); "walk in love" (5:2); and "walk circumspectly" (5:15), to name just a few of the admonitions about their walk. In the book of Acts, the Christian life also is spoken of several times as the "way." In the short distance from the altar to the tabernacle, the priests would get their sandal-shod feet dirty and would need them washed before entering into the holy place to minister. In our walk we sin and get our feet dirty and need them cleansed, so we need the laver, which pictures Christ cleansing us from the world's defilement (1 Jn 1:9).

A wonderful explanation of this principle is in John 13, about foot-washing. When the Lord came to Peter to wash his feet, Peter said, "Thou shalt never wash my feet." Jesus answered, "If I wash thee not, thou hast no part with me" (v. 8). The word for "part" has the idea of fellowship or partnership in activity, nothing of relationship. Peter wanted fellowship; he already had a relationship with Jesus. Therefore he said "Not my feet only, but also my hands and my head" (v. 9). Jesus answered, "He that is washed [or "bathed," as the Greek word *louo* means] needeth not save to wash [Greek, *nipto*] his feet, but is clean every whit" (v. 10). Greek scholars for years have pointed out that the first word for washed is *louo*, which means "to bathe all over." The second is *nipto*, which means "to wash just a part of the body," such as the hands and feet. These words accurately fit the functions of the brazen altar and laver. He that has been bathed from his sins at the altar in salvation does not need to be bathed again, but simply needs to wash his feet at the laver from the defilement of sins before entering the holy place of worship and service. Jesus was showing Peter that He was going to forgive him for the denial even before he committed the act, as foretold in verse 38. Today we practice foot-washing as we "wash one another's feet" (Jn 13:14) when we forgive one another.

Today's message for us is that forgiveness for sins we commit after salvation is already assured and provided for in the laver. God does not want us to sin. "My little children, these things write I unto you, that ye sin not. And if any man sin, we have an advocate with the Father, Jesus Christ the righteous: and he is the propitiation for our sins: and not for ours only, but also for the sins of the whole world" (1 Jn 2:1-2). God would still say, "Go, and sin no more" (Jn 8:11). But, knowing that the spirit of man "indeed is willing, but the flesh is weak" (Mt 26:41), and that man will sin, God says there is provision made for cleansing that sin. Jesus is our Lawyer or Advocate who pleads our case, because Satan, "the accuser of our brethren" (Rev 12:10), will certainly accuse us. How will our Lawyer plead our case? Hebrews 9:26 says He has gone into God's presence with His own blood which He shed once and for all. This is God's sole basis for our atonement and forgiveness, "for the blood of Jesus Christ his Son cleanseth us from all sin" (1 Jn 1:7).

At their consecration the priests were washed by another. "And Moses brought Aaron and his sons, and washed them with water" (Lev 8:6). However, they were to wash themselves at the laver. When we are saved or born again, we are washed by Christ Himself, our High Priest. "Not by works of righteousness which we have done, but according to his mercy he saved us, by the washing of regeneration, and renewing of the Holy Ghost" (Titus 3:5). From then on we are responsible to come to the laver ourselves and wash our own feet, even as "Aaron and his sons shall wash their hands and their feet thereat" (Ex 30:19).

The Procedure for Today

The procedure for us today is given in 1 Corinthians 11:31-32: "For if we would judge ourselves, we should not be judged. But when we are judged, we are chastened of the Lord, that we should not be condemned with the world." This confirms the fact that, when the believer sins, the result is not condemnation with those who have rejected the payment made by Christ. "There is therefore now no condemnation to them which are in Christ Jesus" (Ro 8:1). For the

44

believer, the result of sin is chastening, a spanking, if you please, from the Lord. The unbeliever, the world, will be judged later at the great white throne, but he is "condemned already, because he hath not believed in the name of the only begotten Son of God" (Jn 3:18). That will be his day of execution, and now he only dwells in the death cell, as it were. The believer is judged right away, either by himself or by the Lord. If the Lord has to judge him now, it will be via weakness, sickness, or death (1 Co 11:30).

Look at Hebrews 12:4-11 to understand something of the Lord's chastening: "For whom the Lord loveth he chasteneth, and scourgeth every son whom he receiveth" (v. 6). God chastens us, His children, because He loves us and does not want us ruined by sin. God does not merely give out advice. His Word says, "He that spareth his rod hateth his son" (Pr 13:24). God "chasteneth . . . every son whom he receiveth," for still "there is none righteous, no, not one" (Ro 3:10). If one who professes to be a believer goes on in sin and is not chastened of the Lord, it is because he is not really saved at all, not a child of God, according to Hebrews 12:8. God's chastening is always for our own good, and "it yieldeth the peaceable fruit of righteousness unto them which are exercised thereby" (v. 11).

"Furthermore we have had fathers of our flesh which corrected us, and we gave them reverence: shall we not much rather be in subjection unto the Father of spirits, and live?" (v. 9). Notice these two words at the end: "and live." God said Aaron and his sons were to wash at the laver "lest they die." It is repulsive for a child not to be in submission to his earthly father, but it is much worse for a child of God, who has been redeemed from his sins at such tremendous cost, not to submit to God's chastening. God will not stand for that. God's child can come to the point of hating God's reproof and thereby commit the "sin unto death," and God will take his life, for "he that hateth reproof shall die" (Pr 15:10). What other explanation can be given for these two words: "and live"? This "sin unto death" of 1 John 5:16 is that of a believer, and the death must be physical. Since God chastens through death, as shown in 1 Corinthians 11:30 and many other examples in the Bible, this must be the result and explanation of these verses. It is a serious thing to get out of fellowship with God and face His chastening.

The way to escape His chastening is to judge ourselves. We simply must examine our lives and our motives daily. When the Holy Spirit shows us sin, we must deal with it. First John 2 says we can judge ourselves when we "walk in the light" (1:7). We do this by feeding daily on God's Word and allowing the Holy Spirit to throw light on our actions and attitudes. "If we say that we have no sin, we deceive ourselves, and the truth is not in us" (v. 8), but when we become conscious of our sin and "we confess our sins, he is faithful and just to forgive us our sins, and to cleanse us from all unrighteousness" (v. 9). This is washing at the laver. We are not to come as some do, saying, "We have not sinned," and thereby "make him a liar" (v. 10), but we are to name the sin to God and trust Him to forgive it that very moment.

Now, it is one thing to confess sin and another to ask God to forgive you all your sins. Many come saying glibly, "God, forgive us of our many sins." They have not confessed a thing and will not get the peace and forgiveness they desire. This is a deep truth and the reason many believers no longer have the joy of their salvation. We must keep good records with the Lord. Just as David acknowledged and confessed his sin and asked God to restore the joy of his salvation (Ps 51:12), so we must confess in order to get the joy we once knew.

The ultimate purpose of the laver was for the priests to cleanse themselves so they could go into the holy place. Inside the holy place were the food for the priests or the shewbread, the altar of incense or place of prayer, and the candlestick. These represent spiritual exercises and worship for the believer. The reason most people do not enjoy praying or worshiping the Lord is that they are on the outside, out of fellowship with Him. It is such a serious thing that God warned them twice that they should wash "that they die not"

(Ex 30:20). We are under grace today, and God does not kill every believer who comes into His presence in an attempt to worship with unconfessed sins, but His mercy does not make it less wrong.

5

The Sustenance of the Shewbread

Our baby boy had no concern for his mother and father, for at two o'clock in the morning he cried until he had awakened us. He did not care how tired we might be or how much trouble it caused us: he wanted his two-o'clock bottle. Needless to say, we got up and gave it to him.

God says, "As newborn babes, desire the sincere milk of the word, that ye may grow thereby" (1 Pe 2:2). God's Word is the food that a Christian needs for growth. He should cry out for it with hunger pains if not fed, just as a baby cries for its milk. The shewbread in the holy place was the priest's food.

The table of shewbread was three feet long by one and one-sixth feet wide and two and one-third feet high,—a rather small table. It, too, was made of acacia wood, but it was covered with gold and not brass. Around the top was a rim to hold the bread from falling off. Also, it had rings of gold and staves of wood covered with gold by which the priests could carry it on their journey. Dishes, spoons, and bowls to be used in making the bread were also made of gold. Twelve small cakes or loaves of bread were made each Sabbath and put on the table for a memorial before the Lord.

The Purpose of the Shewbread

The purpose of the shewbread was to provide for the priests' food (Lev 24:9). The priests were given much other food to sustain their physical bodies, but this food was for them to eat as they officiated in the tabernacle in worship and service for God. This eating was done as an act of worship

49

and spiritual fellowship with the Lord. No doubt this spiritual food was eaten in deep contemplation of the Lord's presence in the tabernacle.

The believer's spiritual food is God's Word, both the written Word and the living Word, the Lord Jesus, as revealed in the written Word. Milk is to be fed to the "babe," but "strong meat belongeth to them that are of full age" (Heb 5:14). Jeremiah said, "Thy words were found, and I did eat them; and thy word was unto me the joy and rejoicing of mine heart" (Jer 15:16). Job declared, "I have esteemed the words of his mouth more than my necessary food" (Job 23:12b). The more we behold "the glory of the Lord" in the Word of God "with open [unveiled] face," we are "changed into the same image from glory to glory, even as by the Spirit" (2 Co 3:18). As we study God's Word, we need to look for the Lord Jesus on every page and, as we see Him, become more like Him. To disect God's Word and become theologically correct in our doctrine is not enough. It should not be an end in itself, though we should leave no stone unturned to be correct in doctrine, for the Word should have an effect upon our lives or we will come short of the glory of God!

The Place of the Shewbread

Let's learn some lessons from the shewbread by seeing first the *place* in which it was eaten: "in the holy place" (Lev 24:9). This was the first room inside the tabernacle proper, the covered part. It is the place of fellowship with the Lord. It meant they had been to the brazen altar, that they were saved. They also had passed the laver and washed thereat "lest they die," which meant confessing sin and cleansing from defilement since they left the brazen altar, corresponding to the believer confessing his daily sins and being in perfect fellowship with the Lord. Inside the holy place, with no unconfessed sin, they could have fellowship with the Lord and partake of spiritual food.

Could these truths explain why many of God's children do not feed on the Word of God? They are out of fellowship with the Lord; they are outside the tabernacle, needing their feet and hands cleansed from defilement. Sin in the life will ruin the appetite for God's Word, for sin will keep you from the Word or the Word will keep you from sin. The reason some people get so much from the Word and have fresh truths to teach others is that they are in fellowship with the Lord and spend time in His presence feeding on His Word.

The only way the priests could see to eat the shewbread was by the light from the lampstand. When a man says he reads the Bible but gets nothing out of it and cannot understand it, he is confessing that he is still a natural man, because "the natural man receiveth not the things of the Spirit of God: for they are foolishness unto him: neither can he know them, because they are spiritually discerned" (1 Co 2:14). "Now we have received, not the spirit of the world, but the spirit which is of God; that we might know the things that are freely given to us of God" (1 Co 2:12). The believer, in fellowship with God in the holy place, can know God's Word and understand it, for the Holy Spirit is there to show him the Word.

In the holy place, the priest was shut out from the world and its distractions. Inside was the place of perfect peace so he could enjoy fellowship at the Lord's table. When one spends time in the holy place in fellowship with the Lord, the world will have no attraction for him. Inside the holy place, all furnishings were made or covered with gold, which must have been a beautiful sight. The spiritually minded person, spending time in the holy place, sees some of the Lord's beauties. The gold speaks of God's royal presence. The acacia wood covered with gold speaks of Jesus' humanity covered with God's deity. Outside the holy place, the acacia wood covered with brass pictured Jesus suffering as a man for our sins. His perfect humanity took our sins upon Him, and He died in our place. Inside the holy place, the humanity and deity are seen combined, with the deity overshadowing His humanity and shining forth. At the brazen altar the deity is hidden from human sight and we see Him judged in our place.

Today many people only see Jesus' humanity. At Caesarea Philippi, Jesus asked, "Whom do men say I the Son of man am?" (Mt 16:13). The disciples answered, "Some say that thou art John the Baptist: some, Elias; and others, Jeremias, or one of the prophets" (v. 14). Those observers saw only the human characteristics that paralleled the men they named. When Jesus asked, "But whom say ye that I am?" (v. 15), Peter, seeing beyond Jesus' humanity, said, "Thou art the Christ, the Son of the living God" (v. 16). His knowledge came from spiritual insight given by God the Father. Inside the holy place we see the Lord Jesus Christ, in whom "dwelleth all the fulness of the Godhead bodily" (Col 2:9).

The Position of the Shewbread

A second important thing about the shewbread is its *position*, for the table was only a little over two feet high, making it accessible only to a bending or kneeling person. The Word of God is also accessible to a person who humbles himself. How thrilling that even a babe in Christ can find precious morsels in it, and can make the promises real and practical in his life. How wonderful are these words of Jesus: "I thank thee, O Father, Lord of heaven and earth, that thou hast hid these things from the wise and prudent, and hast revealed them unto babes" (Lk 10:21). He added, "Blessed are the eyes which see the things that ye see; for I tell you, that many prophets and kings have desired to see those things which ye see, and have not seen them" (vv. 23-24). So today, spiritual babes in Christ who humble themselves before the Lord and spend time in His presence are illumined to see things in the Word of God that even those of great intellect cannot see without the Spirit. We should praise Him for the spiritual understanding He gives, and then humble ourselves before Him, for we see higher on our knees in His presence at the table of shewbread than at any other place.

The Priests and the Shewbread

The *priests* were to eat of the shewbread, as "it shall be Aaron's and his sons'" (Lev 24:9). This spiritual food was for those who worshiped and served the Lord. Today God says that every believer is a priest, for we are "a royal priesthood" (1 Pe 2:9). Revelation 1:6 (NASB) says the Lord Jesus "has made us to be a kingdom, priests to His God," which means the Word of God is meant for every believer to feed upon personally. A believer needs no one but the Holy Spirit to interpret God's Word to him: "But the anointing which ye have received of him abideth in you, and ye need not that any man teach you" (1 Jn 2:27). There is no excuse for the Christian not knowing God's Word, for God is anxious and willing to feed all who come to the table and help themselves. Aaron and "his sons" were to eat it. It is the most natural thing for children to follow in the footsteps of their father.

The Prescription for the Shewbread

The *prescription* for the shewbread (Lev 24:5) said it was to be of "fine flour." As the fine flour was used in making the meal offering which is a type of Christ, here again it is the picture of Christ, the living Word of God. There were no eggs or sugar, just the fine flour. We need the simple Word of God today *with nothing added*. Some try to dilute or destroy God's Word, but we just need to take God at His Word and act upon it. There should be no alterations of the Word, for God's Word is "settled in heaven" (Ps 119:89), and He has exalted it above His name.

The Portion of the Shewbread

The *portion* was given as "two tenth deals" in each cake (Lev 24:5). One-tenth was the amount in an omer, which was the daily portion of manna for the children of Israel. So there was more than enough in each cake for a priest. There were twelve cakes, so each name represented on the priest's breastplate had a full supply.

The Partaking of the Shewbread

There must be a *partaking* of the shewbread, for, "they shall eat it" (Lev 24:9). It was not enough to merely look upon or to handle the shewbread; it had to be eaten. Bibles are in profusion in America today, but too few persons feed upon the Word. It matters not how beautiful or how prominent the Bible is in a home; it must be read and digested if it is to do any good. The sad commentary of Jeremiah 6:10b is too true today: "Behold, the word of the LORD is unto them a reproach; they have no delight in it." Hours spent watching TV or reading newspapers are sad excuses for not having time for the Word. Perhaps more than anything else, television is the reason that many "have no delight in" God's Word, for it destroys the appetite for spiritual food. Also, it takes time to digest and assimilate food. We must spend time in the holy place, in fellowship with the Lord, to see Jesus and digest the spiritual food of the Word. Joshua says we should "meditate therein day and night" on the Word of God (Jos 1:8). As a cow chews its cud, so we should "meditate" on the Word, chewing on it until we thoroughly digest it. We feed on the Word when we allow it to grip our hearts. As we read it, we should enter into its truths and experiences until they affect our lives. Psychologists say people are using movies and TV as escapisms; they project themselves into the actors' experiences until they get a measure of satisfaction from feeling as though they have had the same experience. In a very real sense we should project ourselves as though we have partaken of the experiences of God's people in all their victories, and claim by faith the same power and purposes they had in order to do great exploits for God. We are told, "Whatsoever things are true . . . pure . . . lovely," etc., to "think on these things" (Phil 4:8). We naturally think or meditate on the things we have seen or heard or read about recently. The Bible says, "Set your affections on things above" (Col 3:2) and "think on these things." So we must spend time reading and feeding on God's Word, which is our special food as God's priests.

Have you ever noticed that many couples begin to look alike after they have lived together for years? Similarly, as we see the "glory of the Lord" in His Word, we will be "changed into the same image" (2 Co 3:18). "We would see Jesus" (Jn 12:21) is the cry of our hearts today. We can see the Lord Jesus on every page of His Word if we "eat" it in the holy place.

6

The Intercession at the Altar of Incense

Incense, once widely used in homes to rid them of musty and unwanted odors, is made from certain dried fruits, flowers, bark, woods, gum resins, and "sweet spices" (Ex 30:34). Two of the three gifts brought by the wise men to the Lord Jesus were frankincense and myrrh, two kinds of incense. When it was burned it smoldered slowly, sending up smoke of a pleasant fragrance that permeated the air.

In the holy place was "an altar to burn incense upon" (Ex 30:1), which was eighteen inches square and only three feet high. It stood in front of the veil inside the tabernacle. Horns extended from its four corners, just as on the brazen altar. Made of acacia wood, it was covered with pure gold. Around the top was a rim or crown to keep the incense from falling off the edges. Like the other furniture, it had rings and staves in the sides by which to carry it. A specific recipe was given for making the incense, which was to be used only in the tabernacle in the Lord's service.

The Picture of Prayer

The psalmist said, "LORD, I cry unto thee: make haste unto me; give ear unto my voice, when I cry unto thee. Let my prayer be set forth before thee as incense; and the lifting up of my hands as the evening sacrifice" (Ps 141:1-2). Here is another tabernacle "figure" which has cast many shadows of truth we can rejoice in and profit from today. The psalmist

57

connected incense and prayer; the ascending of incense was the way he wanted his prayer to go up before God. He wanted his prayer to be as fragrant and pleasant to God as incense. Incense, then, was a picture of prayer in Old Testament days.

The New Testament also uses incense to picture prayer. In Revelation 5:8, "The four beasts and four and twenty elders fell down before the Lamb, having every one of them harps, and golden vials [censers] full of odours [incense], which are the prayers of saints." Here the incense is stated to be prayers, and not just a picture of prayer.

Revelation 8:3-4 reads,

> And another angel came and stood at the altar, having a golden censer; and there was given unto him much incense, that he should offer it with the prayers of all saints upon the golden altar which was before the throne. And the smoke of the incense, which came with the prayers of the saints, ascended up before God out of the angel's hand.

The smoke of the incense was offered with the saints' prayers, and the two came together before God. Not only is incense a picture of prayer here, but the two are aligned. They are given as one and the same thing in Revelation 5:8. Incense, then, speaks of prayer ascending up before God, certainly a sweet smell to Him.

The altar of incense teaches us much about prayer. Here we can find out how to get our prayers answered. Many people never get their prayers answered; the tabernacle can show us why this is true. There are more instructions and information about prayer in the altar of incense than in any other place in the Bible. If you want to know how to get your prayers answered and what may be hindering your prayers, you can find the answer at the tabernacle and at the altar of incense.

The Place of Prayer

One of the first lessons about prayer from the altar of incense is the place of prayer. God said, "And thou shalt put it before the vail that is by the ark of the testimony, before the mercy seat that is over the testimony, where I will meet with thee" (Ex 30:6). This, we know, was in the holy place just before the veil which stood between the holy place and the Holy of Holies where God dwelt with His people. To offer the incense the priest had to be inside the holy place at the place of worship.

There are two prerequisites for anyone coming into the holy place and to the altar of incense. First, he had to go to the brazen altar where the animal was slain and the blood shed. The brazen altar, the place of sacrifice, was the picture of Calvary and of Christ suffering, dying, and shedding His blood for our sins. No one dared enter the holy place without the blood having been shed. Today this means that anyone who wants to pray must first of all be sure that he has been to Calvary, where by faith he has offered Christ as his Saviour, as his Substitute and sacrifice for sins. He must claim Christ's blood to cleanse him from all sin before he can ever come into God's presence. An unsaved person has no access, no right, to come into God's presence in prayer and expect anything. The first prerequisite, then, is that a person must be saved or be born again. He must have sacrificed the Lamb of God for himself (when he claimed Jesus as his personal Saviour by faith).

Maybe you have prayed over and over again and wondered why God never heard your prayers and why you never got an answer. Perhaps the reason is that you have never personally received Christ as your Saviour. To receive answers to prayer, a person must first of all be saved. He must have a sacrifice before he can come into God's presence. Hebrews 10:19-20 says, "Having therefore, brethren, boldness to enter into the holiest by the blood of Jesus, by a new and living way, which he hath consecrated for us, through the veil, that is to say, his flesh." God invites us to "come boldly unto the throne of grace, that we may obtain mercy, and find grace to help in time of need" (Heb 4:16). But we do not come without the blood, without having claimed Christ's blood to cleanse us, to allow us to stand in the presence of a holy God.

The second prerequisite for coming to the altar of incense is in Exodus 30:18-20, where God said,

> Thou shalt also make a laver of brass, and his foot also of brass, to wash withal: and thou shalt put it between the tabernacle of the congregation and the altar, and thou shalt put water therein. For Aaron and his sons shall wash their hands and their feet thereat: when they go into the tabernacle of the congregation, they shall wash with water, that they die not.

The priests had to wash their hands and feet before entering the holy place to worship, to offer incense to the Lord. This was so essential that God said they had to do it "lest they die." We saw that the laver is the place of confession of sin for the believer before he can come into God's presence to worship or serve Him. He must be cleansed from the daily defilement of sin. "If I regard iniquity in my heart, the Lord will not hear me" (Ps 66:18). This is another reason why some believers never get their prayers answered. We should be washed before we can pray to God, for He will not hear us with unconfessed sin in our lives, and our prayers will go unanswered.

Some today who have grudges, envy, jealousy, and animosity in their hearts are cheating themselves from seeing victory in their lives and from seeing God answer their prayers. "The eyes of the LORD are upon the righteous, and his ears are open unto their cry. The face of the LORD is against them that do evil" (Ps 34:15-16). God says we should pray (Lk 18:1) and that He is a God who hears prayer (Ps 65:2), but the prayer must come from those who have been washed—who are saved and have confessed their sins—before they come into His presence. Not just the unregenerate have "the face of the LORD . . . against them," but so do His own children who are walking in disobedience with unconfessed sin. To have our prayers answered, we must go to the laver and confess and forsake every sin.

Could this be why you have not had your prayers answered? Is there some inward, secret sin, known to no one but you and God, that is hindering your prayers? Confess it to God and forsake it; then come boldly to the throne of grace, and you will find "help in time of need" (Heb 4:16). Some have prayed for divine healing of their bodies, others have asked for power to witness, while still others have asked for better jobs, better health, and finances, but all has been in vain simply because there is still unconfessed sin in their lives.

God is a holy God, and the priest stood in the holy place to come to Him, for there he was in the place of fellowship with God. There he was occupied only with spiritual things and worshiped the Lord. This is the place where prayer ascends to God and gets through to Him. To get our prayers answered we must spend time in fellowship with God. "If ye abide in me, and my words abide in you, ye shall ask what ye will, and it shall be done unto you" (Jn 15:7). This takes time. It means shutting ourselves up alone with God, spending time alone with Him in prayer, fellowshiping with Him, delighting ourselves in the Lord. It means to "set your affection on things above, not on things on the earth" (Col 3:2). This is talking about sitting together in "heavenly places in Christ Jesus" (Eph 2:6). We have been raised into the heavenlies; but only as we enjoy this fellowship and spend time there in spiritual things will we see God answer our prayers. A person can be in fellowship with another person, but, because they are hundreds of miles apart, they are not having fellowship with one another. We may be in fellowship with God, having no unconfessed sin in our life, yet we do not spend time in the holy place, fellowshiping with Him. Therefore, we do not get whatever we ask of the Lord. We need to abide, to dwell, and to spend time in God's presence to get our prayers answered:

Being in the holy place also depicted being in God's will. When God told the priests to go into the holy place, He said, "And thou shalt make an altar to burn incense upon" (Ex 30:1). It was God's will for the priests to go in and offer up incense. To get our prayers answered we, too, must be in God's will, and we must pray in His will. "And this is the confidence that we have in him, that, if we ask any thing according to his will, he heareth us: and if we know that he hear us, whatsoever we ask, we know that we have the petitions that we desired of him" (1 Jn 5:14-15). Until a person has learned to pray in God's will and according to God's will, he will not see his prayer answered. There must be submission in the heart and mind of the believer when He prays. If the Lord Jesus is our Example, as He is, then we also need to be able to pray from the depth of our heart, "Not my will, but thine, be done" (Lk 22:42b). We must subject our personal desires, ambitions, pleasures, and everything else to God's perfect, sovereign will so that we will trust God "that all things work together for good to them that love" Him (Ro 8:28). If we get our prayers answered, it must be according to God's will, in the holy place, in fellowship with God, with no unconfessed sin in our lives.

The Position of Prayer

The position of the altar of incense was "before the vail that is by the ark of the testimony, before the mercy seat" (Ex 30:6). Since the altar of incense was two cubits high, while the Mercy Seat was a cubit and a half high, at the altar of incense one looked down upon the Mercy Seat. In the Old Testament, there was a veil between the altar of incense and the Mercy Seat. But the veil has been rent in two (Mt 27:51). We can come boldly to the throne of grace, directly into God's presence, and look on the Mercy Seat. As we come to God in prayer, we need to realize that we come to a throne of grace and whatever we receive is because of God's mercy. We deserve nothing; we should have a deep sense of our unworthiness before God. For one to demand anything of God indicates that he certainly is not conscious of looking on the Mercy Seat. We are indeed "heirs of God, and joint-heirs with Christ" (Ro 8:17); but while we are still in the flesh, there should be a deep consciousness of our unworthiness before God. God said, "If my people, which are called by my name, shall humble themselves, and pray, and seek my face, and turn from their wicked ways: then will I hear from heaven" (2 Ch 7:14). "God resisteth the proud, but giveth grace unto the humble" (Ja 4:6). The proper position for prayer is not a matter of standing, kneeling, with the head bowed or lifted up, but it is the attitude of the heart in a conscious looking upon the Mercy Seat, upon God's grace and goodness, so undeservingly received from Him.

The Power of Prayer

God instructs that the horns of the altar of incense shall be of acacia wood (Ex 30:3), overlaid with gold. Horns in the Bible speak of power. Daniel 8:6-7 speaks of the power of the ram with two horns. After the horns were broken (v. 7), "there was no power in the ram." Two articles in the tabernacle had horns on them: the brazen altar, reminding us that there is power in the blood to cleanse from all sin, and the horns on the altar of incense, speaking of power in prayer, not in the prayer itself but in the One to whom the prayer is directed. God has ordained to use prayer to work miracles for His saints. The horns came out of the altar, not out of the incense. The altar, made of acacia wood covered over with gold, speaks of Christ. The brazen altar speaks of Christ in His humanity, judged for our sins, while the golden altar or altar of incense, made of acacia wood and covered over with gold, speaks of Christ glorified.

Christ is our Advocate; our prayer must go through Him to the Father. He is our Intercessor who "ever liveth to make intercession for us" (Heb 7:25) at the Father's right hand. There is power in prayer directed to God through Christ. If we have the "faith as a grain of mustard seed" (Mt 17:20), we can say to a mountain, "Be thou removed" (Mk 11:23), and it will. James says, "Is any among you afflicted? Let him pray" (5:13). He tells us further that "the prayer of faith shall save the sick, and the Lord shall raise him up" (v. 15). There is power in prayer over physical sickness and ailments, so that

God can intervene and work in our behalf. How tragic that so few today truly avail themselves of this power and see God work miracles in answer to prayer, to raise up the sick or afflicted. The power of prayer is summed up in James 5:16b: "The effectual fervent prayer of a righteous man availeth much." The availing is limited only by how much we pray.

With these promises in prayer and the power of prayer, no wonder James said, "Ye have not, because ye ask not" (4:2b). For one of God's children to go through life and not avail himself of this mighty weapon of warfare simply means he is cheating himself and living a beggarly life when he could live a rich life. Too often prayer is a last resort, when it should be the first. We say, "I can't do anything else to help you, but I will pray," as though this were an extremity when nothing else will avail. God help us to realize the power in prayer and use it to its fullest for His glory!

Exodus 30:10 says, "Aaron shall make an atonement upon the horns of it once in a year with the blood of the sin offering of atonements: once in the year shall he make atonement upon it throughout your generations: it is most holy unto the Lord." In prayer the saint pleads for no blessing and asks for no pardon that His blood has not already bought.

The Provision for Prayer

The lampstand with its light was in the holy place so that the priests could see as they ministered at the altar of incense. Offering the incense was connected with lighting and dressing the lamps both in the morning and evening. "And Aaron shall burn thereon sweet incense every morning: when he dresseth the lamps, he shall burn incense upon it. And when Aaron lighteth the lamps at even, he shall burn incense upon it" (Ex 30:7-8). The only way the priest could see when offering the incense was by the light of the lampstand.

Today God has made provision for the believer in prayer in the person of the Holy Spirit, who gives light, instruction, and illumination in spiritual things. "In the same way the

Spirit also helps our weakness; for we do not know how to pray as we should, but the Spirit Himself intercedes for us with groanings too deep for words" (Ro 8:26, NASB). The Holy Spirit shows us how to pray; He helps us to know what to pray for, and He Himself makes intercession for us. Multitudes of believers have testified that in times of deep distress, when they neither knew how to pray nor for what to pray, somehow it seemed as though, just by groaning from their hearts, the burden of their hearts ascended to God. They sensed that God heard the unvoiced prayer. There is real comfort in realizing this help from the Holy Spirit. Ephesians 6:18 tells of "praying always with all prayer and supplication in the Spirit." Prayer is to be in the light shed by the Holy Spirit, in His power and energy, directed and assisted by Him. This is the divine provision for prayer to teach us how to pray, and also to know for what we should pray.

The Person of Prayer

The altar of incense was to be put "before the vail that is by the ark of the testimony" (Ex 30:6). Without a doubt, as the priests came into the holy place to offer the incense they were aware that just beyond the veil was the Mercy Seat where God dwelt with His people. They must have been conscious of how close they stood to His very presence. To come directly into His presence, they would have to go through the veil. Later the veil was "rent in twain" (Mt 27:51), so we can come directly into God's presence as we pray today. This veil (Heb 10:20) represented Jesus in His flesh, and He is the High Priest over God's house through whom we draw near "with a true heart in full assurance of faith" (v. 22). In a very real sense we come to God's throne. We come in Jesus' name, through Him, and Him alone. The Lord Jesus said, "Whatsoever ye shall ask the Father in my name, he will give it you" (Jn 16:23). Prayer is made through Christ Himself. We do not come to God through Mary, the saints, angels, or anyone else, but through Christ. To get our prayers answered, we must be sure that we come to God in prayer in

Jesus' name, for He is the One who endorses all our prayers. If you would go to a bank and sign your name to a multimillion-dollar check without any money behind it, you would receive nothing. If we go to God in prayer in our own merit, we will get nothing. We need to come through the person of Jesus Himself, not just tacking "for Jesus' sake" or "in Jesus' name" on the end of our petitions, but in reality coming in His name.

The Practice of Prayer

"And Aaron shall burn thereon sweet incense every morning: when he dresseth the lamps, he shall burn incense upon it" (Ex 30:7). When is the best time to pray? God instructed Aaron to offer incense every morning. Every believer will admit it is good to pray in the morning when his mind is fresh and clear, uncluttered with the day's affairs. The Bible starts out, "In the beginning God." We too should begin every day with God. We need instruction and inspiration to face the day; we know not what the day may hold, but we know who holds the day.

A good example is given in Psalm 5:3, "My voice shalt thou hear in the morning, O LORD; in the morning will I direct my prayer unto thee, and will look up." Many great saints of God found the early morning hours, when all is quiet and one can be alone, the best time to spend with God in prayer. Christ set an example in Mark 1:35, "In the morning, rising up a great while before day, he went out, and departed into a solitary place, and there prayed." For us to find a solitary place, it is almost a must that we get up early. If we wait until later in the day, we may find ourselves so rushed from one essential duty to another that we shove prayer aside and never find time to pray as we should.

Another good time is mentioned in Exodus 30:8, "And when Aaron lighteth the lamps at even, he shall burn incense upon it." It is a good thing to stop at the end of the day and look back over its events and count your blessings and praise God for them. Someone has said, "To thank God for our blessings extends them; not to thank Him ends them." Prayer is not always just asking for something; it should be filled with thanksgiving. Evening is a good time when we can thank God for all He has done for us throughout the day. One sign God gives of the last days is that people shall be unthankful (2 Ti 3:1). Also, in the evening we should judge ourselves (1 Co 11:31). If we were to do this regularly and confess our sins to Him, we would not be judged or chastened of the Lord, as so often is the case. We are told, "Let not the sun go down upon your wrath" (Eph 4:26).

Many can testify, "My soul shall be satisfied as with marrow and fatness; and my mouth shall praise thee with joyful lips: when I remember thee upon my bed, and meditate on thee in the night watches" (Ps 63:5-6). In the evening we should pray ourselves to sleep, which will bring satisfaction to our souls. If many who are bothered with insomnia would learn to meditate upon God at night, their whole lives would be enriched and transformed. A preacher often gets some of his best messages and sermons as he lies in bed at night, meditating upon God's Word and praying for the services to come. We are told to "stand in awe, and sin not: commune with your own heart upon your bed, and be still" (Ps 4:4). To get our prayers answered, to be relieved of the agonizing burdens of our hearts, to see miracles in answer to prayer, maybe we need to confess: "I am weary with my groaning; all the night make I my bed to swim; I water my couch with my tears. Depart from me, all ye workers of iniquity; for the LORD hath heard the voice of my weeping" (Ps 6:6, 8).

The Persistence of Prayer

There must be persistence in prayer. "A perpetual incense before the LORD throughout your generations" (Ex 30:8). This immediately reminds us that we should "pray without ceasing" (1 Th 5:17). We should pray in the morning and in the evening, but we also should be in a constant attitude of prayer all day long. Moment by moment, as the need arises, the smoke of our incense should ascend to God

67

all through the day; no matter where we are. Christ, even on the cross, amid all the jeering and scoffing, prayed to God. We need to develop the habit of prayer so that at the very moment of need we can cry out to God from hearts that stay in tune with Him. It was said of Charles Spurgeon that he glided from laughter to prayer with the ease of one who lived in both elements. He was always in touch with God, so it was as natural for him to pray as to breathe. This is praying without ceasing. Nothing is too trivial or too great to bring to God, so pray without ceasing.

The Passion of Prayer

The incense was made to ascend by burning. "And Aaron shall burn thereon sweet incense every morning" (Ex 30:7). This reminds us that "the effectual fervent prayer of a righteous man availeth much" (Ja 5:16b). Sometimes we sense that our prayers do not get any higher than our heads. If we were to search our hearts honestly we would have to admit that our prayer at that moment was not a deep burden or conviction of our heart. Sometimes, too, we know our heart is not right toward God as we pray. Also, there are times when we are conscious of deep need; we are greatly moved by the urgency of the matter and cry out of broken hearts to God. This is the burning of incense, the effectual fervent prayer that ascends to God.

Cheap, trumped-up, sentimental emotionalism won't get a thing from God, but the person who comes to Him with a broken heart, a broken and a contrite spirit, shall be effectual and receive answers. When Hannah was deeply moved as she prayed to God for a son, she said, "I have . . . poured out my soul before the LORD" (1 Sa 1:15). In prayer like that, one is not so much conscious of the phrasing of his petitions as he is of communicating his burden to God and crying out for help. Where is brokenness of spirit today? Where do you hear praying out of broken hearts? How long has it been since someone prayed and you felt as though God were right there? When did you feel as though the person reached up and got hold of God Himself as he cried in agony and a broken spirit for God to hear and answer him? It isn't that our tears or our agony change God's heart and mind, but our passion simply tells us that our hearts are so in tune with God that we can pray in His will, "Not my will, but thine, be done." We are praying in the Spirit, so we can receive the petitions we ask of God. As we look at the world in sin and see men and women about to perish, we need to get stirred up and cry out to God about these things. Effectual, fervent prayer will go up as incense and reach the throne of God to get our prayers answered.

The Prescription for Prayer

And the LORD said unto Moses, Take unto thee sweet spices, stacte, and onycha, and galbanum; these sweet spices with pure frankincense: of each shall there be a like weight: and thou shalt make it a perfume, a confection after the art of the apothecary, tempered together, pure and holy: and thou shalt beat some of it very small, and put of it before the testimony in the tabernacle of the congregation, where I will meet with thee: it shall be unto you most holy. And as for the perfume which thou shalt make, ye shall not make to yourselves according to the composition thereof: it shall be unto thee holy for the LORD. Whosoever shall make like unto that, to smell thereto, shall even be cut off from his people (Ex 30:34-38).

This incense was made of precious and rare ingredients, each of the same weight and importance. God warned that the people were never to make anything that smelled like it, for this incense was only to be made to offer up to God. These three spices in no way typify or represent three things in prayer, but there are three specific factors for getting our prayers answered. First, prayer is to be made in Jesus' name, for He said, "Hitherto have ye asked nothing in my name: ask, and ye shall receive, that your joy may be full" (Jn 16:24). Again, "And whatsoever ye shall ask in my name, that will I do, that the Father may be glorified in the Son. If ye shall ask any thing in my name, I will do it" (Jn 14:13). One of the prerequisites of prayer is that we pray in Jesus' name, not just for His sake, but consciously in His name.

Second, we must pray believing, for God said, "And all things, whatsoever ye shall ask in prayer, believing, ye shall receive" (Mt 21:22). "He that cometh to God must believe that he is, and that he is the rewarder of them that diligently seek him" (Heb 11:6). An essential ingredient in prayer is to come believing that God hears prayer and that He is a prayer-answering God. A good practice is to make a list of our requests and, after we have prayed for them, to mark down the date of the answer. Many never expect to see God work miracles in answer to prayer, and because of their lack of faith they never get their prayers answered.

A third ingredient for prayer is that we pray in His will. "And this is the confidence that we have in him, that, if we ask any thing according to his will, he heareth us: and if we know that he hear us, whatsoever we ask, we know that we have the petitions that we desired of him" (1 Jn 5:14-15). Prayer is to be in God's will, according to His will, for Him to answer our prayer.

In all three of these instructions God makes blanket statements that whatsoever we ask, we will have. For results, we need to be sure prayer has these three ingredients.

The Perversion of Prayer

After God had given the prescription for prayer, He warned, "Ye shall offer no strange incense thereon" (Ex 30:9). There was to be no perversion of the offering of the incense. Anything offered other than what God had prescribed was "strange incense," a perversion of what He had instructed. The word "strange" in Hebrew means "alien" or "foreign," so anything offered that was not in accordance with God's prerequisites was alien or foreign. Jesus warned, lest our prayers be as that of the hypocrites, that we should not pray to be seen or heard of men, and not to make vain repetitions as the heathen do. Those practices are "strange incense." To read a prayer from a prayer book simply be-

70

cause we think it is pretty, when it has not become our own from our heart, is certainly strange incense not prescribed by God. Many times in churches people pray aloud with high-sounding phrases and clichés they have heard from others, and we become more conscious of what they are saying than to whom they are praying. Praying to be heard of men can easily become the strange incense we are warned not to offer.

What would a mother think if her little child came and read to her a flowery statement by someone else, as though it were her own request? The mother would rather have her come and just say what she wants, out of her heart in her own words. Whether flowery and high-sounding or not, this would be real and not foreign to her. The best way to pray is to come with open, bared hearts, sincerely before God, and simply make our requests known to Him. God is not so much concerned with the words and the way we express them as He is with the earnestness of our hearts and our coming in faith, believing. We need to be sure that our prayer is our own, from our heart, prescribed by God, ascending to Him. Any other prayer is strange incense forbidden by God.

The Prompting of Prayer

Nadab and Abihu offered strange fire before the Lord, and God killed them because of it.

> And Nadab and Abihu, the sons of Aaron, took either of them his censer, and put fire therein, and put incense thereon, and offered strange fire before the Lord, which he commanded them not. And there went out fire from the Lord, and devoured them, and they died before the Lord" (Lev 10:1-2).

They were doing a right thing, but in the wrong way. They were the sons of Aaron and had a right to offer incense. God does not tell us where they got the fire, but He does say it was "strange fire . . . which he commanded them not." Because of their disobedience, God destroyed them with fire.

In Leviticus 16:12 the fire to be used in the censer to offer up incense was to come from the burning coals of fire on the brazen altar. That which was to kindle the incense and cause it to ascend to God was to come only from the brazen altar; anything else was strange fire. "And there came a fire out from before the LORD, and consumed upon the altar the burnt offering and the fat: which when all the people saw, they shouted, and fell on their faces" (Lev 9:24). Here we see the origin of the fire which God wanted used to offer not only the sacrifices, but also the incense. It was fire from the Lord Himself that consumed the sacrifice. When the people saw the sacred and unusual fire, they shouted and fell on their faces. When the Lord Jesus died on the cross 1,900 years ago, the Bible says "it pleased the LORD to bruise him" (Is 53:10). Men did not put the Lord Jesus to death, but God laid upon Him the iniquity of us all and caused Him to suffer. It was the fire of God, the judgment of God, that came upon Him for man's sin. This is why He was consumed. This is why He died.

What, then, should cause us to pray today? What should make the incense ascend from our hearts? Too many people claim they need to get inside an ornate church, with soft music, to put themselves "in an atmosphere and mood of prayer." External means to prompt prayer are nothing more than "strange fire." One motivation to cause incense to arise from our hearts is a look at the wondrous cross of Calvary. Fire, or prompting, from God for what the Lord Jesus has done for us, should make us pray. We do not need the external means and methods of man; we simply need to keep close to Calvary.

Paul said he wanted to glory in nothing "save in the cross of our Lord Jesus" (Gal 6:14). If we do glory in the cross—not just a metal ornament about our necks or a statue with the image of Christ upon it—and with the eye of faith look back at Calvary and see what the Lord Jesus did for us, we will have all the burden, all the urge, we need to pray. Perhaps this is why the Lord's Supper is important for us today. Jesus said, "This do in remembrance of me" (Lk 22:19b). As we partake of the Lord's Supper we are reminded of His death, sufferings, and the shedding of His blood, and we do show His death until He comes. When we come to the Lord's table and there truly remember His death, we have a hunger to pray. The incense is ascending up from our heart at that time, and this is a delight to God. Prayer that is prompted by anything else is "strange incense," and God says it brings forth death; it is an abomination to Him. As believers, we should be careful not to lean on external means to motivate prayer. It may be strange fire that comes forth, and, instead of our getting our prayers answered, we might receive God's wrath.

The People for Prayer

When the priests went into the holy place to worship God they were to put on a "breastplate of judgment." In this breastplate were twelve precious stones, each engraved with the name of one of the children of Israel. A beautiful picture is given in Exodus 28:29-30,

> And Aaron shall bear the names of the children of Israel in the breastplate of judgment upon his heart, when he goeth in unto the holy place, for a memorial before the LORD continually. And thou shalt put in the breastplate of judgment the Urim and the Thummim; and they shall be upon Aaron's heart, when he goeth in before the LORD: and Aaron shall bear the judgment of the children of Israel upon his heart before the LORD continually.

The priests were reminded that they were continually bearing the names of people upon their hearts before the Lord. This certainly is the way prayer should be made by believers. To really get our prayers answered we should have names of individuals upon our heart. It is not enough for us to pray vaguely and generally, "Lord, save everybody" or "God, bless everyone." Often in church we pray, "Lord, if there is an unsaved person here, save him today." Week in and week out, many churches never see one person come to know Christ as personal Saviour.

What a difference when in a church the believers have the

names of individuals upon their hearts and pray specifically, "God, save Bill and Joe." They see them come, one after another, confessing Christ as personal Lord and Saviour. This is true in individual prayer life as well. Those who only pray generally, do not see very many come to Christ. But those who keep a prayer list of individual names that they pray for specifically and consistently, will often find them coming one after another to receive Christ as Saviour. We need to pray for believers too. It is one thing to pray for God to heal all the sick and to bless all the missionaries, but it is far different to pray for individuals by name. It may be time-consuming and may seem repetitious to make the same request for many separate individuals, but this is God's method for answering our prayers. Many missionaries, delivered in a time of deep need or distress, learned later that someone had prayed very specifically for them at the exact moment of deepest need. This is true intercession. We must be specific in praying and bear the names of individuals before the Lord.

It is no accident that the breastplate was to be upon the high priest's heart when he went in before the Lord. This reminds us that prayer must come from the heart. Prayer needs to be fervent; it needs to mean business with God. We do not simply go through the motions of prayer, vainly repeating names or requests, but true prayer comes from the bottom of our hearts. The high priest was to bear the names of the children of Israel upon his heart. When God's people, a church or an individual, bear people upon their heart before the Lord continually, this will bring revival and transform a church in a very real way. Prayer merely uttered from the head because "we should pray" does not often get the answer from God. But prayer upon the heart of a saint who pleads for individuals before the Lord is heard of God, and the answer is given.

If we will bear the names of people upon our hearts before the Lord continually, we will not only see our own lives transformed, but the Church transformed as well. Multitudes will come to know Christ as Saviour. We must deal with people as individuals and not in groups; name them one by one before God, and see God work in their hearts and transform their lives for His glory.

The Preciousness of Prayer

Whatever else might be said of prayer, "It is most holy unto the LORD" (Ex 30:10). Without a doubt God loves to hear His children talk to Him. Parents cherish the memory of their children first beginning to talk and coming to them even with the most minute, insignificant little requests. There is not a sadder moment than when a parent is denied the privilege, either through death or distance, of being able to communicate with his child. If talking to one another is so precious and real to us, how much more must it be between God and His own children. The Bible tells us "it is most holy unto the LORD" (Ex 30:10). God wants us to pray; He wants to hear us talk to Him; He wants to know our burdens and sorrow. It delights Him to hear us tell Him the requests of our hearts, that He as our heavenly Father might do something about them.

God was greatly provoked as they were "burning incense unto other gods in the land of Egypt" (Jer 44:8). Not only did they burn incense to other gods, but they burned incense unto the "queen of heaven" (vv. 17-19, 25). This, of course, God forbids, for incense is holy and precious to the Lord. To offer up prayer to anyone other than God Himself is an abomination and is disobedience unto God. Prayer is "most holy unto the LORD" (Ex 30:10). May we keep it that way in all our practice, that there be no perversion of our offering of incense to the Lord.

7

The Light at the Lampstand

In many mansions and castles of old, often the first and most dazzling thing to strike the eye was a magnificent chandelier. Thousands of dollars were spent on these ornate ceiling fixtures but not for their beauty alone; the light from them was essential. In God's tabernacle, no less importance was placed upon the light inside.

The Picture of the Lampstand

The lampstand was made of pure gold beaten by the skillful hands of the craftsman whom God had filled with wisdom (Ex 31:1-11). Six branches came out of the sides of the main shaft. Each of the branches and shafts was exquisitely beaten, with flowers and knobs, and with an almond-shaped bowl at the end to hold the oil and wicks. The lampstand was made of a talent of gold.

Notice in Exodus 25:31-32, God says, "And thou shalt make a candlestick of pure gold . . . his shaft, and his branches, . . . And six branches shall come out of the sides of it [the shaft]." We are not left to our own imagination as to the typology of the "lampstand." In Revelation 1:12, John was shown "seven golden candlesticks." The Lord Jesus, whom He saw at this time, gave him the secret of this vision: "The seven candlesticks which thou sawest are the seven churches" (v. 20b). As we look at the candlesticks or lampstands in detail we can easily see the Church represented. It had one main shaft with six branches coming out of its sides. Christ obviously is represented by the shaft, and the Church by the branches. Christ is elsewhere described as the vine, and we are the branches coming out of the vine; or He is the Head, and we are the body joined eternally to the Head. The lampstand is another picture of our union with Christ.

We need not be surprised to find a picture of the Church in the tabernacle, for a number of types of the Church are either indicated or implied in the Old Testament. Several types of the Church as a bride are in the Old Testament, such as the bride of Isaac, Rebekah, and the Gentile bride of Joseph in Egypt. No doubt these were not recognized as types of the Church at the time, any more than Abraham realized his offering of Isaac was a type of Christ being offered up. Nevertheless, here is a beautiful and complete picture of Christ and His Church.

Six is the number of man. The Church of the Lord Jesus Christ is made up of ordinary human beings united with Christ through His shed blood. We are many members differing from one another, but all essential and important to the body if it is to function properly. By themselves, the branches of the lampstand had no standing in the tabernacle. Today, apart from Christ, we have no standing before God. One is the number of unity, deity, and sovereignty. The single shaft represented Christ, to whom we are united by the new birth and work of the Holy Spirit. The shaft and branches joined together made the perfect number, seven. The branches with the shaft are complete. We "are complete in him, which is the head of all principality and power" (Col 2:10).

The Plan for the Lampstand

"Thou shalt make a candlestick of pure gold . . . and his branches . . . shall be of the same" (Ex 25:31). The gold in the tabernacle represented Deity, for here we see much of Deity. The shaft representing Christ was of pure gold, for "the Word was God" (Jn 1:1). When Christ said, "He that hath seen me hath seen the Father" (Jn 14:9), it was not just a figure of speech, for He was "God . . . manifest in the flesh" (1 Ti 3:16). In the brass outside the tabernacle we saw the sufferings of

78

Christ, and now in the gold we see "the glory that should follow" (1 Pe 1:11). Here is true Deity.

The branches were to "be of the same." Does that mean we are divine, too? In part now, at least. "Whereby are given unto us exceeding great and precious promises: that by these ye might be partakers of the divine nature" (2 Pe 1:4). Make no mistake about it; this is a reality. People ask, "How can I live the Christian life?" You have a new nature, a new set of desires—divine desires from a divine nature. You will "do what comes naturally." We are definitely a "new creation" with a new nature, even partaking of the "divine nature." We are now "sons of God" by this new birth into God's family. We have the same kind of life, eternal life, as the Lord Jesus, and because He lives we shall live and never die! It is true we are still in this body of humiliation, but when He comes for us we shall be changed. When we see Him, we shall be like him, not only in nature, but completely. What a glorious day that will be!

The Procedure for Making the Lampstand

What was the procedure for making the lampstand? "Of beaten work shall the candlestick be made: . . . all it shall be one beaten work of pure gold" (Ex 25:31, 36). In chapter 32 the golden calf was molded. What is idolatrous and designed by man can be easily and quickly cast into shape, but the lampstand was beaten into shape only from divine wisdom and with great effort. "He was wounded for our transgressions, he was bruised for our iniquities: the chastisement of our peace was upon him; and with his stripes we are healed" (Is 53:5). "For Christ also hath once suffered for sins, the just for the unjust, that he might bring us to God, being put to death in the flesh, but quickened by the Spirit" (1 Pe 3:18). Salvation is free, but is is not cheap, for we were "bought with a price" (1 Co 6:20). Now "we are his workmanship, created in Christ Jesus unto good works" (Eph 2:10). "Unto you it is given in the behalf of Christ, not only to believe on him, but also to suffer for his sake" (Phil 1:29).

For us to be molded and shaped into the instruments God would have us to be so that He might be able to use us to full advantage, we are to be "beaten" even as the shaft was. It may not be with the stripes of the cat-o'-nine-tails, but God has His ways of fashioning us, some through fire, some through deep sorrow, but "thou shalt remember all the way which the LORD thy God led thee these forty years . . . to humble thee, and to prove thee, to know what was in thine heart, whether thou wouldest keep his commandments, or no" (Deu 8:2). Remember, we are of "one beaten work." We cannot be separated from the shaft. We can no more perish than can the Lord Jesus when we are "in" Christ and of "one beaten work."

The Purpose of the Lampstand

The lamps were to be lit "that they may give light over against it" (Ex 25:37). Any lampstand has one main purpose: to give light. Christ, as the shaft, said, "As long as I am in the world, I am the light of the world" (Jn 9:5). A primary purpose of Jesus was to be "the light of men" (1:4). "And the light shineth in darkness; and the darkness comprehended it not" (1:5). As we look back now and see the blaze of light He brought to reveal God and eternal life to men, we wonder how, when they saw His miracles and life, they did not comprehend or lay hold of it. God explains it to us when He says men are "dead in sins" (Eph 2:5); "their minds were blinded" by Satan (2 Co 3:14). They had "the understanding darkened, being alienated from the life of God through the ignorance that is in them, because of the blindness of their heart" (Eph 4:18).

There were some who saw, for Peter said, "Thou art the Christ, the Son of the living God" (Mt 16:16). Jesus told Peter, "Flesh and blood hath not revealed it unto thee, but my Father which is in heaven" (v. 17). It should humble us before the Lord to realize the grace of God that our eyes are open to see the light and to know Christ as our Saviour.

Not only did the main shaft have a bowl at the end of it, but each branch had a bowl and light at its end. These bowls had oil and a wick in them that made the light. The oil is a type of the Holy Spirit and is discussed later. The wick pictures the life of each believer as he burns out for God. Jesus said that, while He was here, He was the light of the world; but now that He is gone, His words, "Ye are the light of the world" (Mt 5:14), are in effect. What a responsibility is ours to take His place in the world!

Jesus stated further in the same passage, "A city that is set on an hill cannot be hid. Neither do men light a candle, and put it under a bushel, but on a candlestick; and it giveth light unto all that are in the house" (vv. 14b-15). Do you give light to all who are around you? Just as there was a difference about the Lord Jesus and His life, that those around Him knew that He was a "teacher come from God" (Jn 3:2), so men should be able to tell by our lives and actions that we are "born of God" (1 Jn 5:1).

The admonition now is to "let your light so shine before men, that they may see your good works, and glorify your Father which is in heaven" (Mt 5:16). Every child of God has a light, a testimony, which he is to allow to shine. To hide it by putting it under a "bushel" is abnormal. The light shines through his good works, done not to attain salvation, but because he is saved. He must be sure his works done "before men" (Mt 6:1) are not done for the praise of men, else he would then have his reward; they should be done to glorify God. His motives must be pure, for Christ knows them and they shall be revealed at His judgment seat (1 Co 3:13; 4:5).

As a group of believers in a local church, you, too, have a testimony or a lampstand. If this testimony is not burning brightly, or if you let the "lamp of God" go out (1 Sa 3:3) in your assembly because of sin, God "will remove thy candlestick out of his place" (Rev 2:5). Too many individuals have no testimony for Christ and, sadly, many churches where once the fires of revival burned and the light of God shined, now have "Ichabod," which means "the glory is departed," written over them. We need old-fashioned heart-searching to see if we have not left our "first love" and we must "repent, and do the first works" (Rev 2:4-5). If a church can go for weeks on end with no one brought "out of darkness into his marvellous light" (1 Pe 2:9), there should be some real soul-searching. "The way of the wicked is as darkness: they know not at what they stumble" (Pr 4:19). But, praise God, we *do* know, and we must show them in love and compassion. "In the midst of a crooked and perverse nation, . . . ye shine as lights in the world; holding forth the word of life" (Phil 2:15).

The Plan for Lighting

"They shall light the lamps thereof" (Ex 25:37). There is human responsibility for the light to be lit and burning. The priests were to light the lamp. God's plan is to use men as they preach the Word of God for people to come out of darkness into the light. "There was a man sent from God, whose name was John. The same came for a witness, to bear witness of the Light, that all men through him might believe" (Jn 1:6-7). As Christ is seen through us, and as we give out the Gospel, we light the lamps in men's lives all over the world. By preaching and exhortation, we fan the flame in men's lives, exhorting "one another daily, while it is called To day; lest any of you be hardened through the deceitfulness of sin" (Heb 3:13).

The individual is also responsible to "draw nigh to God" (Ja 4:8). What a sad day in Israel when Isaiah could say, "And there is none that calleth upon thy name, that stirreth up himself to take hold of thee" (Is 64:7). The need of the hour is for us to take stock of our own lives and then shake and stir ourselves out of our own lethargy. "Go to the ant, thou sluggard" (Pr 6:6). "Awake to righteousness, and sin not; for some have not the knowledge of God: I speak this to your shame" (1 Co 15:34). These admonitions of a gracious God exhort us to action before He has to chasten us into action the hard way. Since we are all priests, we should beware lest the lamp of God go out in our own lives.

The Preparation of the Lamps

"And the tongs thereof, and the snuffdishes thereof, shall be of pure gold" (Ex 25:38). The tongs were used to trim the wicks so the lamp would not flicker and go out. We must trim our lamps daily, as they did in the tabernacle, if our testimony is to be what it should. Bob Gray, pastor of the Trinity Baptist Church of Jacksonville, Florida, suggests that the "snuffdishes," or "boxes," were used to preserve the burned-out wicks, and that perhaps in the true tabernacle in heaven God is storing them for a special memorial before Him. Even as a sparrow does not fall to the ground without God knowing it, a man never burns out for God but what special note is taken. Far away by yourself, never making headlines, living sacrificially, burning out for God, remember the "snuffdishes" where the wicks were not thrown on the ground, but saved in golden boxes. All the trimming of our life is done with golden tongs with the loving care of our heavenly Father.

Now, a wick is not to be seen but only to burn to allow the light to shine. When the light goes out, the wick is seen. This is true in life today. When we are burning for Christ, we are not seen; His glory is seen through us. When our light shines so men see our works and glorify us, we have missed the boat. The real light of God, our testimony, has gone out and the reward is the praise of men, not of God.

The Cause of the Light

God told the Israelites to bring "pure oil olive beaten for the light, to cause the lamp to burn always" (Ex 27:20). The lampstand, though beautiful, was useless without oil to burn in it. The wick would not produce light without oil, so the oil was essential above all else. Oil throughout the Scriptures symbolizes the Holy Spirit; here we see how essential He is if, individually or collectively, we are to have a light shining for Christ. The disciples were powerless until the day of Pentecost, when the Holy Spirit came upon them and they received power and became witnesses of Christ. The essential difference between the Christians of the first century and today is the filling of the Holy Spirit. They fasted while we feast, they prayed while we play, and they were filled with the Holy Spirit while too often we are filled with a hateful spirit or a careless spirit. Nothing will cause the light to burn but the oil. Nothing is going to set our churches or ourselves on fire for God but the emptying of self and the filling of the Spirit. Not our enthusiasm or endeavors but the energizing of the Holy Spirit will cause a life to shine for Christ.

Israel's responsibility was to fill the lamps with oil. God always is ready to fill the vessel that contains the "treasure" of the Gospel (2 Co 4:7), and the formula is that we "draw nigh to God, and he will draw nigh" to us (Ja 4:8). The priests could have had the most perfect wick possible, but it would not burn without oil. All the training, talents, and efforts in the world will not get the job done without the oil, the Holy Spirit. Our testimony as a Christian or as a church will shine only as the Holy Spirit is allowed to flow in and through us and "cause the lamp to burn."

The Command of God

"Thou shalt command the children of Israel, that they bring thee pure oil olive beaten for the light, to cause the lamp to burn always" (Ex 27:20). Though obviously the oil was essential to cause the light to burn, God said, "Command the children of Israel" to bring the oil. This is a picture of the Christian being filled with the Holy Spirit, so the filling of the Holy Spirit is a command of God. Ephesians 5:18 says, "Be not drunk with wine, wherein is excess; but be filled with the Spirit." This is not optional; it is a divine imperative.

Too many today are totally oblivious to the Holy Spirit in their lives. They know nothing of His work in and through them. Many do not want to pay the price of a Spirit-filled life. It means giving up too much of self and the desires of the flesh, and they treat this command as though they have an option to refuse to yield to the Holy Spirit. As God admonished Moses to command the children of Israel, so we as God's ministers are to command the children of God to be filled with the Holy Spirit. Not to do so is rebellion and sin.

The Clean Oil

Notice in Exodus 27:20 that it was to be pure oil or, as the Hebrew word means, *clean*. There were to be no impurities, lest they hindered the light from burning. There was to be no mixture, only the pure oil. So today, if we are to shine for the Lord, there must not be any impurities in our life that would grieve the Holy Spirit. We are told, "Grieve not the holy Spirit of God" (Eph 4:30). Above all else, the Holy Spirit is *holy*. Any impurity in our lives grieves Him who is so designated. The reason so many lose the consciousness of His peace and presence is that they allow so-called little things in their lives. With all the jealousy, envy, strife, and hate among the saints, no wonder there is little power in the average church. The Holy Spirit has to work *on* the believer to convict him of sin, instead of *through* him to convert sinners. When David sinned and acknowledged it, he asked God to restore the joy of His salvation (Ps 51:12). If you lack the joy you once knew as a child of God, perhaps you, too, have grieved the Holy Spirit. Praise God, you can have peace and joy restored when you confess the sin the Holy Spirit is putting His finger on right now, for "if we confess our sins, he is faithful and just to forgive us our sins, and to cleanse us from all unrighteousness" (1 Jn 1:9).

Constant burning of the oil

The oil was to "cause the lamp to burn always." This was to be a *constant* burning. It was not enough for the lamp to burn brightly one day and be quenched the next. God was so concerned in Samuel's day that "ere the lamp of God went out in the temple of the LORD, . . . the LORD called Samuel" (1 Sa 3:3-4). Another admonition of God for us is to "quench not the Spirit" (1 Th 5:19). Any urge, yearning, or desire we may ever have had for spiritual things, God put there and wants us to respond and not to quench the Holy Spirit.

Remember, "it is God which worketh in you both to will and to do of his good pleasure" (Phil 2:13). What a sacred thing that God should give us even one desire to please Him! The reason people don't read the Word or pray or witness is that they don't want to. If there is one desire in your heart to please God, be assured that He put it there; and God help us if we quench that desire.

Apart from the Holy Spirit, "there is none that seeketh after God" (Ro 3:11). When you first came to Christ, you longed to see loved ones and friends come to Him. What has happened to that desire? I do not know all that the verse means when God says, "Unto every one that hath shall be given, . . . but from him that hath not shall be taken away even that which he hath" (Mt 25:29). But one thing is definite: the context tells us that if God gives us anything and we do not use it, we will lose even that. If God gives us the desire to witness, and we quench the Spirit by not responding in obedience, we will lose that desire. These are sobering, solemn facts we should consider seriously.

Continual filling of the lamps

It was not enough for the lamps to be filled once; God said, "Aaron and his sons shall order it from evening to morning before the LORD" (Ex 27:21). When the tabernacle was first set up, no doubt they filled the lamps and may have foolishly felt that was enough and left the lamp alone. God said they were to fill the lamps morning and evening; once for all was not enough to keep the light burning. Similarly, we need a continual filling of the Holy Spirit. It is too bad some interchange the New Testament terms of "being baptized" and "being filled with the Holy Spirit." Worse yet is to argue over the expression and miss the experience of being filled with the Holy Spirit. The book of Acts tells of the disciples being filled with the Holy Spirit over and over. This is the enabling, energizing, and empowering work of the Holy Spirit in the believer's life for service. Too many, like Samson, do not know that they are not filled with the Holy Spirit and go out powerless to defeat (Judg 16:20-21). For our light to shine, we must have a continuous filling of the Holy Spirit.

8

The View at the Veil

"Warning! Do Not Enter!" There was no such sign on the veil, but God had given His instructions. The priests knew that they were not to enter beyond it into the Holy of Holies. Only the high priest was allowed to do so, and then just once a year.

The veil divided the two rooms inside the tabernacle. The first room, called the holy place, contained the three pieces of furniture discussed in the previous chapters. The other room was called the "holiest of all," or "the Holy of Holies." Inside the Holy of Holies was kept the Ark of the Covenant, above which God said He would commune with the high priest, who represented His people (Ex 25:22). In the Holy of Holies the Shekinah glory was to be seen—the manifest presence of God. The veil hid this sight of God; it was the final step into the presence of God.

The Description of the Veil

The *description* of the veil is in Exodus 26:31: "And thou shalt make a veil of blue, and purple, and scarlet, and fine twined linen of cunning work: with cherubims shall it be made" (Ex 26:31). Immediately one can see it is the same as the outer court gate (27:16). That gate was a picture of Christ, the blue represented Him in His heavenly character as the Son of God come down from heaven; the purple, the color of royalty, depicted the Lord Jesus as the King of the Jews who one day will be recognized as King of kings and Lord of lords; the scarlet portrayed Him as the Lamb of God who shed His blood for our sins; and the fine linen of His righteousness.

Hebrews 10:19-20 says something particular about this veil: "Having therefore, brethren, boldness to enter into the holiest by the blood of Jesus, by a new and living way, which he hath consecrated for us, through the veil, that is to say, his flesh." This veil was a picture of Jesus in His flesh; all this was true of Him from the day He was born—when "God sent forth his Son, made of a woman" (Gal 4:4).

We have boldness now to enter into the presence of God, into heaven itself, through the veil, that is, through Christ and what He did in the flesh. Jesus said, "I am the way" and "no man cometh unto the Father, but by me" (Jn 14:6).

The Deposit Behind the Veil

Exodus 26:33 tells what was *deposited* behind the veil: "That thou mayest bring in thither within the vail the ark of the testimony." Tremendous things were there: the Ark of the testimony, which held "the golden pot that had manna, Aaron's rod that budded, and the tables of the covenant" (Heb 9:4). These objects were testimonies to the true and living God, and the reason this Ark was called "the ark of the testimony." The manna testified to God's provision in the wilderness, Aaron's rod that budded testified to God's power to bring life from the dead, the tables of the Law testified to God's perfect standard which demanded righteousness for anyone to stand before Him.

Also behind the veil "the glory of the LORD filled the tabernacle" (Ex 40:34), because God dwelt above the Mercy Seat between the two cherubim (25:22).

Jesus' flesh was the veil that hid the glory of God from human eyes. Those who looked beyond the veil of His humanity saw more than a mere man. When Jesus asked, "Whom do men say that I the Son of man am?" (Mt 16:13), Peter looked beyond His flesh and declared, "Thou art the Christ, the Son of the living God" (v. 16). Many today make Jesus a great Teacher or Example and do not see Him as He really is—the divine Son of God.

The Division by the Veil

Look at the *division* by the veil: "And the vail shall divide unto you between the holy place and the most holy" (Ex 26:33). The veil permitted limited access to God, but it also prevented access to Him until it was rent in two. Christ's earthly life was not an example to get us into heaven; His death opened the way.

The veil divided the place of worship and service from God's presence. For any worship to reach God, it must pass through Christ. Much prayer may be made, but it must be in Jesus' name in order to reach God. Many desire to approach God, but they will not get through to Him unless they go through the "one mediator between God and men, the man Christ Jesus" (1 Ti 2:5).

The Disjunction of the Veil

The *disjunction* of the veil as told in Matthew 27:51-52, says,

> And, behold, the veil of the temple was rent in twain from the top to the bottom; and the earth did quake, and the rocks rent; and the graves were opened; and many bodies of the saints which slept arose, and came out of the graves after his resurrection, and went into the holy city, and appeared unto many.

The veil was only a curtain and not a wall. God tells us "the way into the holiest of all was not yet made manifest" (Heb 9:8). Not until Christ's death was the way manifest and opened into God's presence. First notice that it was *divinely rent* in two: the picture of Christ's death. They were simultaneous. The veil was rent in two "from the top to the bottom" (Mt 27:51), not by man but by God. Tradition says this veil was four inches thick, and two teams of oxen hitched to each side could not tear it apart. Obviously no man could. Jesus said, "No man taketh it [My life] from me, but I lay it down of myself" (Jn 10:18). The men of Jesus' day were simply God's instruments to carry out His divine plan of redemption. Isaiah said, "It pleased the LORD to bruise him" (53:10). On Calvary, God was judging our sin in the person of His Son "who his own self bare our sins in his own body on the tree" (1 Pe 2:24).

The veil was *dramatically rent*. "The earth did quake, and the rocks rent; and the graves were opened" (Mt 27:51-52). With many who came out of their graves appearing in the city, there could be no question about it being known that something unusual had happened. Those who witnessed it had no excuse for their unbelief. God did all that was needed to show them that Jesus Christ had fulfilled prophecy and was the Messiah.

The veil was *deliberately rent*. The way to God is now opened completely for all. God says we can "come boldly unto the throne of grace" (Heb 4:16), and we have "boldness to enter into the holiest by the blood of Jesus" (10:19). Without the rent veil we could not have such access.

9

The Ark

Preparation of the Ark

Directions for the Ark's preparation are given in Exodus 25:10-15. This chest was three feet nine inches long, two feet three inches wide, and two feet three inches high, making it about the size of a small cedar chest. It was made of acacia wood with an overlay of "pure gold, within and without" (v. 11). Four rings of gold were on the sides to hold staves of wood, also covered with gold, by which to carry the Ark on the Israelites' journeys through the wilderness. The Ark's top was a slab of solid gold called the Mercy Seat, with two cherubim at the ends, all made of one piece of beaten gold. The cherubim faced each other, with their wings stretched out over the Mercy Seat and touching each other. Here, God said, "I will meet with thee, and I will commune with thee from above the mercy seat, from between the two cherubims which are upon the ark of the testimony" (Ex 25:22).

The command for the Ark's construction

Note God's command: "And they shall make an ark of shittim wood" (v. 10). The way to approach God and the place to meet Him come as a revelation from Him, not from the reasoning of man. "There is none that seeketh after God" (Ro 3:11) except by the divine "drawing" of the Holy Spirit (Jn 6:44). Man left to his own devices and wisdom will change "the glory of the uncorruptible God into an image made like to corruptible man, and to birds, and fourfooted beasts, and creeping things" (Ro 1:23). The tragedy is that,

91

with all his wisdom and logic, man cannot realize his folly in turning to false gods, as God says in Isaiah 44:14-19.

Noah was commanded, "Make thee an ark of gopher wood; rooms shalt thou make in the ark, and shalt pitch it within and without with pitch" (Gen 6:14). Reason said this was foolishness, for it had never rained and there was no place to float such an ark. But "by faith Noah, being warned of God of things not seen as yet, moved with fear, prepared an ark to the saving of his house; by the which he condemned the world, and became heir of the righteousness which is by faith" (Heb 11:7).

One other ark is mentioned in Scripture, the ark made by Moses' mother when she hid him from Pharaoh's death penalty upon all Israelite children. She covered this ark with pitch, even as Noah did; the Hebrew word root for "pitch" is also the root for "redemption."

The construction of the ark

The construction of the Ark is given; it was to be made of "wood." This speaks of the humanity of Christ, as "a root out of a dry ground" (Is 53:2). If He were no more than a mere man, there would surely be "no beauty that we should desire him" (v. 2). One thing made a difference, however, for God said, "And thou shalt overlay it with pure gold, within and without shalt thou overlay it, and shalt make upon it a crown of gold round about" (Ex 25:11). Christ was a man in every sense of the word, except that He did not sin, but above all, He was "God . . . manifest in the flesh" (1 Ti 3:16). The word speaks of His humanity and the gold of His diety. From this we see "the sufferings of Christ, and the glory that should follow" (1 Pe 1:11). The wood furniture outside the tabernacle proper was covered with brass, which speaks of judgment. In the holy place or "heaven itself" the wood was covered with gold, speaking of glory to follow. Also, there was the "crown of gold round about." One day He shall wear the crown and be rightfully worshiped as the King of kings and Lord of lords.

The carrying of the ark

Carrying the Ark is mentioned next: "And thou shalt put the staves into the rings by the sides of the ark, that the ark may be borne with them" (Ex 25:14). The Ark, to be carried by Israel as they journeyed through the wilderness, assured them of God's presence. Today we journey as pilgrims and strangers through the wilderness of this world; we also are assured of God's presence with us, for our bodies are the temple of the Holy Spirit. The staves (v. 15) were never to be taken out as long as they were still traveling in the wilderness. So, as long as we are in the world, we have the assurance that the Holy Spirit will abide with us (see Jn 14:16).

When the Ark of the Covenant was captured by the Philistines (1 Sa 4), Eli's daughter-in-law gave birth to a son and named him Ichabod, meaning "the glory is departed" (vv. 19-22). Because God plagued the Philistines so severely, they sent the Ark back to Israel, where it remained in the home of Abinadab in Kiriath-jearim. Many years later, when David had established his throne in Jerusalem, he placed the Ark on an ox-drawn cart, contrary to the instructions in Numbers 4, to take it up to Jerusalem (2 Sa 6). During the journey, one of David's men was killed by the Lord when he touched the Ark to steady it. David, fearing the Lord's wrath, would not take the Ark into Jerusalem; therefore, he put it in the house of Obed-edom. It remained there three months, and Obed-edom and his household were blessed by God. Reassured, David had the ark carried up to Jerusalem by bearers, with sacrifices and great rejoicing.

David was so overjoyed that he girded himself with a simple loincloth and danced in front of the procession. His first wife, Michal, was disgusted with him and berated him for his unkingly behavior. He told her that he was willing to humble himself even more in order to celebrate before the Lord, to whom he owed his position as king. As punishment for her scorn, she remained childless to the day of her death.

Today we need to yield to the Holy Spirit, to do all that

He urges us to do "before the Lord," and not be stopped by criticism or scoffing we receive. This is not at all to endorse wild fanaticism or disorderly behavior; but, as Vance Havner said, "Too many go to the ball games and act like a bunch of Comanche Indians, and then come to church and sit like a bunch of wooden Indians." With a heart of love and devotion to the Lord Jesus, controlled and motivated by the Holy Spirit, we should so walk in the Spirit as to do even the unusual to the glory of God.

Preservation of Articles Within the Ark

Look now at the *preservation* within the Ark. "And thou shalt put into the ark the testimony which I shall give thee" (Ex 25:16). Inside the Ark three things were kept as Israel traveled through the wilderness: "the golden pot that had manna, and Aaron's rod that budded, and the tables of the covenant" (Heb 9:4). It is time to see what these things meant to Israel and what they should mean to us today.

The law

First, there were the tables of the Law which God gave to Moses in the mountain. The first tables were broken by Moses when he came down from the mountain and saw that Israel was breaking the Law in worshiping the golden calf (Ex 32:19). God told Moses to "hew . . . two tables . . . like unto the first; and I will write upon these tables the words that were in the first tables, which thou brakest" (34:1). These tables were deposited within the Ark and kept there for years. Deuteronomy 31:24 says that after Moses finished writing the book of the Law, he instructed the Levites to put it in the Ark of the Covenant, "that it may be there for a witness against thee" (v. 26).

Two things are to be learned from all this. First, the Law was ever present to remind Israel that they had sinned and needed the blood-sprinkled Mercy Seat or they would be condemned. Years later, when Josiah was king, the Law was found in the house of God and read. The king was convicted, as were all the people, and they repented, turned to the Lord, kept the Passover again, and saw revival.

Second, the Law within the Ark speaks of Christ, who could say, "I delight to do thy will, O my God: yea, thy law is within my heart" (Ps 40:8). Again, "I do always those things which please him [my Father]" (Jn 8:29). How wonderful it is to realize that "Christ is the end of the law for righteousness to every one that believeth" (Ro 10:4). He came not to destroy the Law but to fulfill it for you and me. Now God looks at us as though we ourselves had kept the Law, for we are now in Christ, and all that He accomplished is credited to us.

The pot of manna

The golden pot of manna also was kept in the Ark. "And Moses said unto Aaron, Take a pot, and put an omer full of manna therein, and lay it up before the LORD, to be kept for your generations. As the LORD commanded Moses, so Aaron laid it up before the Testimony, to be kept" (Ex 16:33-34). The manna was the food God miraculously provided for the Israelites in the wilderness. It was first given when they began to murmur for lack of food and complained to Moses. God gave them specific instructions about gathering the manna daily and not trying to keep any for the next day. Sure enough, some tried to keep it, but it became rotten (16:20). "And the children of Israel did eat manna forty years, until they came to a land inhabited; they did eat manna, until they came unto the borders of the land of Canaan" (v. 35).

Jesus said,

> I am that bread of life. Your fathers did eat manna in the wilderness, and are dead. This is the bread which cometh down from heaven, that a man may eat thereof, and not die. I am the living bread which came down from heaven: if any man eat of this bread, he shall live for ever: and the bread that I will give is my flesh, which I will give for the life of the world. (Jn 6:48-51).

The manna, then, was a type of Christ.

There is the initial act whereby we partake of Christ as the bread of life and receive eternal life. There is also the daily partaking of Him through the written Word for our spiritual food. This cannot be stored up but must be taken daily, even as the Israelites took the manna daily in the wilderness.

A great tragedy occurred along the way. Israel said, "We remember the fish, which we did eat in Egypt freely; the cucumbers, and the melons, and the leeks, and the onions, the garlick: but now our soul is dried away: there is nothing at all, beside this manna before our eyes" (Num 11:5-6). They forgot the slavery, the hard taskmasters, and bondage in Egypt. When they began to complain about God's provision, they wanted to satisfy their fleshly appetites. It is dangerous to look at and set our affections on temporal things, for we, too, will complain and lose our taste for the things of God.

When Israel grew tired of the manna, "The people went about, and gathered it, and ground it in mills, or beat it in a mortar, and baked it in pans, and made cakes of it" (Num 11:8), but still they could not make it satisfying to themselves. Today, some try to "doctor up" God's Word to make it palatable, but it just will not satisfy the worldly minded. The people cried out for meat, and God sent a wind which brought quail from the sea for them to eat. But God said they were to eat it for a month until it came out of their nostrils and was loathsome to them. It did just that, and then God sent a plague upon them. The sad commentary on this whole incident is in Psalm 106:15: "And he gave them their request; but sent leanness into their soul."

Aaron's rod

Aaron's rod that budded was also to be put in the Ark as a testimony. Again we see another story of tragedy in the life of Israel in their wilderness wanderings, recorded in Numbers 16-17. The people were not satisfied with their leaders.

> And they gathered themselves together against Moses and against Aaron, and said unto them, Ye take too much upon you, seeing all the congregation are holy, every one of them,

and the LORD is among them: wherefore then lift ye up yourselves above the congregation of the LORD?" (Num 16:3).

Does this sound familiar to some congregations today? In the first place, Moses did not take this honor on himself; God chose him. The congregation did not act very holy along the way, even though they thought they were holy. Because of their sin and rebellion, God did a most unusual thing to judge Korah and those who followed him.

> The ground clave asunder that was under them: and the earth opened her mouth, and swallowed them up, and their houses, and all the men that appertained unto Korah, and all their goods. They, and all that appertained to them, went down alive into the pit [hell], and the earth closed upon them: and they perished from among the congregation (vv. 31-33).

It is still a dangerous thing to rebel against God and His leaders!

To show the others who was to be the spiritual leader, God told them to take twelve rods and write the name of the twelve tribes of Israel on them, with Aaron's name on the one for the tribe of Levi. They were to place them before the Ark overnight, and in the morning the owner of the rod that blossomed was to be the leader. When Moses went into the tabernacle of witness, "Behold, the rod of Aaron for the house of Levi was budded, and brought forth buds, and bloomed blossoms, and yielded almonds" (17:8). Here was God's seal on the one to be His leader and priest. "And the LORD said unto Moses, Bring Aaron's rod again before the testimony, to be kept for a token against the rebels" (v. 10). So it was to be a sign for Israel for years to come of their rebellions and of God's seal on Aaron and his sons as priests of God. Ministers of God need the seal of a life-giving ministry and of souls being saved as they minister the Word of God.

Propitiation over the Ark

God tells about the Mercy Seat in Exodus 25:17-22. A slab of pure gold, the same length and width as the Ark, was the

Ark's cover. Made from the same piece of gold and fashioned at the ends of the Mercy Seat were the cherubim. God said that between these two cherubim and above the Mercy Seat is where He would meet and commune with Israel.

The word for Mercy Seat is the same word translated "propitiation," which means to placate, appease, or make satisfaction. The work of Jesus Christ is seen as the fulfillment of the Mercy Seat:

> My little children, these things write I unto you, that ye sin not. And if any man sin, we have an advocate with the Father, Jesus Christ the righteous: and he is the propitiation for our sins: and not for ours only, but also for the sins of the whole world (1 Jn 2:1-2).

Now, God is a holy God, for the seraphim cry, "Holy, holy, holy, is the LORD of hosts" (Is 6:3). Any sin is a heinous offense to God's holiness. Divine justice demands that sin be fully punished, for in no way can an infinite God be generous or lenient toward man in forgiving his sins. The righteous demands of God's Law must be fully met before God can have anything to do with sinful man. However, God's matchless love has provided the one and only way that God can remain just and yet justify the sinner, and that is at the Mercy Seat. Christ has satisfied God's every demand for righteousness and the righteous settlement of man's sins. Christ has once suffered for sins and shed His blood.

In the Old Testament, on the Day of Atonement the priest went into the Holy of Holies and sprinkled the blood of the sacrifice on the Mercy Seat. This was to make atonement for the sins of the people for the past year. When Christ died, "by his own blood he entered in once into the holy place, having obtained eternal redemption for us" (Heb 9:12). "Christ is not entered into the holy places made with hands, which are the figures of the true; but into heaven itself, now to appear in the presence of God for us" (9:24).

Not only was Jesus Christ the atonement for our sins, the sin offering and trespass offering, but He was the fulfillment of the whole burnt offering as well. This was the offering which pictured doing God's complete will and fully satisfying a holy God. It was such an offering that God says is a sweet-smelling sacrifice to Him.

The description of the two cherubim is given in Exodus 25:18-22. From their position they seem to be bowed in the presence of the omnipotent God, indicating an act of reverence. We need to learn from this picture that there should be deep reverence in the presence of the holy God. When the apostle John saw Christ in His glorified form, he "fell at his feet as dead" (Rev 1:17). One day every knee will bow before Him (see Ro 14:11). How tragic that some will have to bow unwillingly and hear the sad words, "Depart from me, ye cursed, into everlasting fire, prepared for the devil and his angels" (Mt 25:41).

Then we see that "toward the mercy seat shall the faces of the cherubim be" (Ex 25:20). The idea seems to be that they are looking on the blood-sprinkled Mercy Seat. First Peter 1:11-12 seems to indicate that Christ's sufferings are "things the angels desire to look into."

Finally, the Mercy Seat is the place of union and communion with God. Man can only meet God on His terms at the blood-sprinkled Mercy Seat. When the sinner comes by faith to the throne of grace and claims Christ's blood to satisfy God for his sins, he will immediately be born of God. This brings him into eternal union with God. No longer is he seen as in Adam alone, for now he is in the second Adam, Christ. No longer is he "without God in the world" (Eph 2:12), but his body becomes "the temple of the Holy Ghost" (1 Co 6:19).

God also says it is from here that He will commune with men from above the Mercy Seat. The tabernacle had a veil which kept the priest from going into the very presence of God except once a year on the Day of Atonement. Now that the veil has been rent, God says we have "boldness to enter into the holiest by the blood of Jesus, by a new and living way, which he hath consecrated for us, through the veil, that is to say, his flesh" (Heb 10:19-20).

10

The Covering of the Cloud

The Glory of God

Moses had such a unique privilege; he talked with God and "the LORD spake unto Moses face to face, as a man speaketh unto his friend" (Ex 33:11). In the course of the conversation Moses made a daring request, "Shew me thy glory" (33:18). God's reply reveals one of the most sacred scenes of the mysteries of God:

> And he said, I will make all my goodness pass before thee, and I will proclaim the name of the LORD before thee; and will be gracious to whom I will be gracious, and will shew mercy on whom I will shew mercy. And he said, Thou canst not see my face: for there shall no man see me, and live. And the LORD said, Behold, there is a place by me, and thou shalt stand upon a rock: and it shall come to pass, while my glory passeth by, that I will put thee in a clift of the rock, and will cover thee with my hand while I pass by: and I will take away mine hand, and thou shalt see my back parts: but my face shall not be seen (33:19-23).

One description of God is "a consuming fire" (Heb 12:29). No wonder Moses could not see Him in His fullness. Because of this, Moses was not ever able to enter the tabernacle (Ex 40:35). It is no wonder that when God appeared to Moses in the burning bush He said, "Draw not nigh hither: put off thy shoes from off thy feet, for the place whereon thou standest is holy ground" (3:5). What Moses did see of God's glory during the days in the mount had a profound effect on him.

"And it came about when Moses was coming down from

101

Mount Sinai . . . that Moses did not know that the skin of his face shone because of speaking with Him. So when Aaron and all the sons of Israel saw Moses, behold, the skin of his face shone, and they were afraid to come near him" (Ex 34:29-30, NASB).

When the cloud was there, God was there. In Revelation 2:1 the Lord Jesus "walketh in the midst of the seven golden lampstands [the churches]." There is a world of difference when you go into a church and can sense God is there. Vance Havner said, "We are too often more conscious of the absence of the people than of this presence of the Lord." There is a glow on the faces of those who are brought into God's presence. It is very real. They are different. They, as Moses, won't boast or be aware of it, but their faces will shine. Others will see it and often be inwardly afraid.

Preachers testify what a difference it makes to stand before a congregation where faces are glowing with the joy of the Lord. He knows he is preaching to people whose hearts are open and responsive: he doesn't have to break through the barrier of hard hearts. A face shows so much A fallen countenance indicates that persons feel that the preacher is preaching *at* them and not *for* them. When Cain sinned, "his countenance fell" (Gen 4:5). Oh, the joy of pastoring a church where God's glory is evident in the people's faces!

This glow, this radiance, this joy that is evident when God really meets with His people, is desperately needed today. Where is the glory of God in the average church? Where are the glowing faces? Where do you sense you are standing on holy ground? Thank God, He is raising up preachers and churches all over the country who are tired of deadness and dryness. They are seeking His face and finding new joy and excitement in His house.

Second Corinthians 3:18 says that as we behold God's glory in His Word, we "are changed into the same image from glory to glory, even as by the Spirit." It is as we are "beholding . . . the glory of the Lord" that we are changed.

Christ must be exalted. In all His beauty and glory He must be preached.

The Goodness of God

The goodness of God is seen in the provision of "the cloud by day, . . . [and] fire by night" (Ex 13:22). It was a wall of protection to the children of Israel as they fled Egypt. When they came to the Red Sea they were stymied. The Egyptians were breathing down their necks, and there was nowhere to go, no place to hide. God put the cloud between the Egyptians and Israel "and it was a cloud and darkness to them [the Egyptians], but it gave light by night to these [Israel] (14:20). It protected Israel from the Egyptians at the rear but provided light for them to go through the Red Sea. How good God is; He still provides protection for His people.

There seems to be another purpose of the cloud, as seen in Isaiah 4:5-6.

> And the LORD will create upon every dwelling place of mount Zion, and upon her assemblies, a cloud and smoke by day, and the shining of a flaming fire by night: for upon all the glory shall be a defence. And there shall be a tabernacle for a shadow in the daytime from the heat, and for a place of refuge, and for a covert from storms and from rain.

Anyone who has been in Egypt and the wilderness between there and the promised land knows how hot the sun's rays can be. Apparently this cloud protected Israel from the blazing heat of the day. The fire must have been their light and heat by night. God thinks of everything. Their shoes never wore out. He provided manna. Above all, He was in their midst all the time. The astounding thing is how Israel murmured constantly in spite of this. The believer today has the admonition, "Let your conversation [manner of life] be without covetousness; and be content with such things as ye have: for he hath said, I will never leave thee, nor forsake thee. So that we may boldly say, The Lord is my helper, and I will not fear what man shall do unto me" (Heb 13:5-6).

The Guidance of God

God guided His people by simply moving the cloud when He wanted Israel to move and then stopping the cloud in the spot He wanted them to abide. God's guidance is so simple, yet so profound.

> And when the cloud was taken up from over the tabernacle, the children of Israel went onward in all their journeys: but if the cloud were not taken up, then they journeyed not till the day that it was taken up. For the cloud of the LORD was upon the tabernacle by day, and fire was on it by night, in the sight of all the house of Israel, throughout all their journeys (Ex 40:36-38).

The children of Israel lived in tents; they were pilgrims who wandered in the wilderness for over forty years. The promised land lay ahead. They lived in a foreign and unknown land. God alone knew the land and what lay ahead, and in His goodness He guided them day by day and step by step. When God was ready for them to move on, He simply lifted the cloud of smoke in the daytime or the pillar of fire at night and moved it in the direction He wanted them to go. If the cloud did not move, Israel dared not move. (See Ex 13:21-22; Num 9:15-23.) From Numbers 9:22 it is evident that Israel stayed only a short time (two days) in certain places, while they stayed "a month" or "a year" at others.

Today God wants to lead His people just as definitely and deliberately by His presence, the Holy Spirit. The Holy Spirit is the One who leads today. "For as many as are led by the Spirit of God, they are the sons of God" (Ro 8:14). "If ye be led by the Spirit" (Gal 5:18).

Now, this is not to strain a point, but perhaps this is why many persons know so little about God's definite leading in their lives. Israel could have ignored the cloud and looked for some other kind of leading from God and missed His will.

There is no jealousy in the Trinity, to be sure, but each Person of the Godhead has a distinct role to play in our lives. Christ, not the Holy Spirit, suffered for our sins. We do not tell lost people about the Holy Spirit. That is simply being discerning and theologically correct.

The Holy Spirit is the One who leads. To ignore the fact that the Holy Spirit leads can cause frustration and many missed blessings of God's leading. Christians need to consciously look to and depend on the Holy Spirit to lead them.

Oh, the joys of walking in conscious dependence upon the Holy Spirit and seeing Him direct your steps to the spot God wants you. One night my wife and I set out to visit for the Lord. Earlier I had felt a deep burden to see someone come to Christ that night. We prayed aloud before we left, asking the Holy Spirit to lead us and to have someone respond. As we were driving toward the first address on our list, I felt an urge to stop for a minute to encourage a man from our church who was having some problems. A couple of weeks before I had taken my travel trailer to his service station to get the electric brake fixed, but he was unable to fix it. That night as we visited, he asked if I had gotten it fixed. I told him two brothers had just opened a station near me and had fixed the brake. Like a flash he asked the brothers' names. I told him one, he blurted out, "I know him. Why, he lives half a block from here. I witnessed to these two brothers and have been concerned about them. I even asked one of my classes to pray for them." When he said that, I felt a strong urge to go by there.

We got the address and went to their door. Barbara, Chuck's wife, came to the door. We introduced ourselves and asked if Chuck was in. He was at work, but, she said, "Do come in." We sat down and began to tell her the great Gospel story about the Lord Jesus. As I told how Christ suffered for our sins, she began to cry. I said, "God has been dealing with you, hasn't He?" She nodded yes. I finished telling her how she could know and receive the Lord Jesus personally. Then

105

she bowed her head and received the Saviour. When we finished praying, the joy of the Lord beamed from her face. We visited about an hour longer, giving her further spiritual instruction.

As we rose to leave, she made the startling statement, "I knew you were coming tonight." Surprised, I said, "Lady, what do you mean, you knew we were coming? You didn't know I existed, and I didn't know you existed. We didn't plan to come here." Then I showed her the names of the people we planned to visit. She replied, "I know all that, but I have been miserable and have prayed all day that God would send someone tonight to tell me how to be saved!"

My wife and I wept, for we felt we were on holy ground. What if we had not been in fellowship with the Lord and had not let the Holy Spirit lead us? We would have missed one of the most thrilling moments of our lives. Yes, God does lead His dear children along today.

There is grave danger in not moving when God leads, but this is also true about moving when God does not lead. When the children of Israel spied out the promised land in Numbers 13 and did not believe the Lord, God said they would not enter the land but wander for forty years. Presumptuously, the people came to Moses and said, "Lo, we be here, and will go up unto the place which the LORD hath promised" (Num 14:40). Moses rebuked them and warned, "Go not up, for the LORD is not among you; that ye be not smitten before your enemies" (v. 42). "But they presumed to go up unto the hill top; nevertheless the ark of the covenant of the LORD, and Moses, departed not out of the camp. Then the Amalekites came down, and the Canaanites which dwelt in that hill, and smote them, and discomfited them, even unto Hormah" (vv. 44-45). What a sad day it was for them. The cloud did not move, the Ark stood still, and Moses departed not, yet the people went on to their own harm and disgrace.

Christians today must live in God's will to avoid many pitfalls and defeats. We need to heed the admonition in James 4:13-15:

106

> Go to now, ye that say, To day or to morrow we will go into such a city, and continue there a year, and buy and sell, and get gain: whereas ye know not what shall be on the morrow. For what is your life? It is even a vapour, that appeareth for a little time, and then vanisheth away. For that ye ought to say, If the Lord will, we shall live, and do this, or that.

It would save many headaches and much loss if Christians would consciously wait on the Lord before making decisions and running out of His will. Many butt their heads against brick walls, totally ignoring God's will.

God's glory, goodness, and guidance are promised for each of us today. The tragedy is the awful famine, dearth, and barrenness of these three things in so many Christians and churches today.

11

The Place of the Priests

The Calling of the Priest

"And take thou unto thee Aaron thy brother, and his sons with him, from among the children of Israel, that he may minister unto me in the priest's office, even Aaron, Nadab and Abihu, Eleazar and Ithamar, Aaron's sons" (Ex 28:1).

God's sovereign call

God said, "Take." Men didn't choose to be priests; they were chosen by God. It has always been so. "And no man taketh this honour unto himself, but he that is called of God, as was Aaron" (Heb 5:4). Men should not decide to become preachers; they must be "called of God." No man should dare to do such a thing, for it is the height of audacity.

Jeremiah knew this sovereign call when he wrote, "The word of the Lord came unto me, saying, Before I formed thee in the belly I knew thee; and before thou camest forth out of the womb I sanctified thee, and I ordained thee a prophet unto the nations" (Jer 1:5). To preach and to suffer as he did, he needed that divine and definite call. "Thou shalt go to all that I shall send thee" (v. 7a). To be sent by God is the greatest of callings. "Whatsoever I command thee thou shalt speak" (v. 7b). To speak what God commands would be to give an awesome message. "Be not afraid of their faces" (v. 8). This boldness is a must for God's servants today also. "Behold, I have put my words in thy mouth" (v. 9). What authority that would give a preacher! No wonder now that we have the Word of God we are commanded to "preach the word" (2 Ti

4:2). This would cause more people to respond to God's ministry today as they did to Jesus: "And they were astonished at his doctrine: for he taught them as one that had authority, and not as the scribes" (Mk 1:22).

Paul knew this sovereign call also, for he said, "But when it pleased God, who separated me from my mother's womb, and called me by his grace, to reveal his Son in me, that I might preach him among the heathen; immediately I conferred not with flesh and blood" (Gal 1:15-16). God chose Paul even before his birth! That should humble any God-called preacher. Then Paul assures us God called him by His grace. No matter who it is, a preacher must know God called him or he will flounder and fail. This call was for two things: First, "to reveal his Son in me." "Holy men of God spake" (2 Pe 1:21), and so those who speak for God today must be holy men of God who reveal Christ in their lives as well as through their lips. Those who preach must be "an example of the believers" (1 Ti 4:12). Preachers must be able to say, "Be ye followers of me, even as I also am of Christ" (1 Co 11:1).

Second, this call was to "preach him [Christ] among the heathen" (Gal 1:16). This is what changes lives of individuals and thus changes the world. Today some are trying to begin with changing man's environment first, but the environment never changes men's hearts. God always changes men on the inside first. The world calls this preaching "foolishness; but unto us which are saved it is the power of God" (1 Co 1:18). Remember, "the gifts and calling of God are without repentence" (Ro 11:29). God never changes. His ways are not man's ways, but they still are the best!

The selective call

Under the Law, God had a severe penalty for anyone who dared to intrude into a priest's office if he were not called to be in that ministry. In Numbers 1:50-51 God specified that the Levites were to be over the tabernacle and to "minister unto it." Then God warned, "The stranger that cometh nigh shall be put to death." The calling of God was selective. The priests were called from among the children of Levi, and no one else dared usurp such authority or ministry.

A very glorious and wonderful thing about this selective calling was that it was to be "from among the children of Israel" (Ex 28:1). Yes, as the song writer said, "He could have called 10,000 angels" to protect Him, and He could have called 10,000 angels to preach about Him, but, thank God, He calls men to minister. As the writer of Hebrews says,

> For every high priest taken from among men is ordained for men in things pertaining to God, that he may offer both gifts and sacrifices for sins; who can have compassion on the ignorant, and on them that are out of the way; for he himself also is compassed with infirmity. And by reason hereof he ought, as for the people, so also for himself, to offer for sins (5:1-3).

The priests were human. "And they truly were many priests, because they were not suffered to continue by reason of death" (Heb 7:23). They were frail and failed too often. God reminds us that "we have this treasure in earthen vessels, that the excellency of the power may be of God, and not of us" (2 Co 4:7) and "that no flesh should glory in his presence" (1 Co 1:29).

Another wonderful side of this calling of men is that "Elijah was a man with a nature like ours, and he prayed earnestly that it might not rain; and it did not rain on the earth for three years and six months" (Ja 5:17, NASB). Many ministers are greatly encouraged by this wonderful fact. It can so easily seem that a man greatly used of God is some superbeing but we all have feet of clay, so we must depend on the Holy Spirit to do everything and be sure that Christ gets the glory.

Some ministers, like Jonah, have run from the Lord. Some may have hid under the juniper tree, as Elijah did. The glorious grace of God is that we can have the wondrous experience of Jonah, "And the word of the LORD came unto Jonah the second time, saying, Arise, go unto Nineveh, that great city, and preach unto it the preaching that I bid thee" (Jon 3:1-2). God doesn't change His mind and withdraw the calling. Maybe you need to hear Him say to you the second time, "Arise, go, preach!"

No wonder God stresses the human element in His servants. Every pastor, every man of God, is still a man at best, and should not "think of himself more highly than he ought to think" (Ro 12:3). On the other hand, God's people should respect God's servants "and . . . esteem them very highly in love for their work's sake" (1 Th 5:13).

The call to serve

The call is to serve, "that he may minister unto me in the priest's office" (Ex 28:1). The priests were not to work at anything else, for this was a full-time job. They were to receive tithes and food from the people. This should be true of God-called ministers today. "Even so hath the Lord ordained that they who preach the gospel should live of the gospel" (1 Co 9:14).

Along with this it should be emphasized that a minister is to minister, to serve. There was hard work, and much work, in the service for the priests. The minstry may look glamorous and easy, but, as any minister worth his salt will tell you, it is taxing and trying, although worth it all. A pastor's wife wrote "Dear Abby," complaining of the inconsiderateness of the people in their parish. She and her husband were disturbed at being called on at all hours of the night. It bothered them that they had so little time of their own. Most pastors count it the greatest honor that people value their prayers at 2:00 A.M. in the middle of a crisis. That kind of pastor knows his calling is to serve.

So high and honored, though, was the priestly ministry that God says, "And the man that will do presumptuously, and will not hearken unto the priest that standeth to minister there before the LORD thy God, or unto the judge, even that man shall die; and thou shalt put away the evil from Israel" (Deu 17:12). The death penalty was upon any who didn't obey the priest. This was under Law, but God says today, "Obey them that have the rule over you, and submit yourselves: for they watch for your souls, as they that must give account, that they may do it with joy, and not with grief: for that is unprofitable for you" (Heb 13:17).

The Clothing of the Priests

Not only is there a calling for God's servants but there is special clothing for them. "And thou shalt make holy garments for Aaron thy brother for glory and for beauty" (Ex 28:2). The special garments for the priest were not ordinary but were expensive and especially designed, as commanded by God. The linen garments entwined with gold, and the breastplate with engraven jewels certainly were beautiful.

The garments were made by those, God said, "whom I have filled with the spirit of wisdom" (v. 3). No one designed his own garment, so there was no rivalry to see who could have the most elaborate or expensive garments. The Holy Spirit gave the directions, and Spirit-filled men conformed by making the clothing exactly as directed.

Today, God's servants are to be clothed with garments of righteousness, as described by the Holy Spirit. Only Spirit-filled men of God will conform as directed.

"And these are the garments which they shall make; a breastplate, and an ephod, and a robe, and a broidered coat . . . and a girdle" (v. 4). When these priests were consecrated, the garments were put on in the order given in Exodus 29:5-6.

The embroidered coat of fine linen was the first garment put on the priest after he was washed at his consecration (Lev 8:7). It was the innermost garment. The ephod, girdle, breastplate, robe, and miter were all embellishments or accessories for the service of the priests. The word for "coat" probably comes from a verb meaning "to cover or hide." Thus the priest was fitted for his holy office by reason of his garments. These dignified his person, covering him with a glory and beauty which he did not possess in himself.

The priests, of course, were only types and pictures of

Christ, the true High Priest. Also, the fine linen is a picture of righteousness (Rev 19:8). Jesus was righteous indeed in birth and behavior. Pilate said, "I find no fault in him" (Jn 19:6). Pilate's wife spoke of Him as "that just man" (Mt 27:19). Stephen called Him "the Just One" (Ac 7:52). Peter tells us He "did no sin" (1 Pe 2:22), and John says, "In him is no sin" (1 Jn 3:5). The statements about the Lord Jesus are summed up in Hebrews 7:26, where He is said to be "holy, harmless, undefiled, separate from sinners."

God's servant today, part of "a royal priesthood" (1 Pe 2:9) who "must give account" (Heb 13:17) for those to whom he ministers, must first be robed with the robe of righteousness provided by God (Ro 3:22). This takes place at his new birth. In his behavior he also must be "blameless" (1 Ti 3:2), "separate" (2 Co 6:17); and "purge himself" to be "a vessel unto honour" (2 Ti 2:21) to be used of the Lord. The Church doesn't necessarily need more men in the ministry, but it does need more "men of God" in the ministry. Not "holier than thou" but "holy" men. "Holy men of God spake as they were moved by the Holy Ghost" (2 Pe 1:21) in former times, and much happened. So it will be today for the man clothed with righteousness.

"The robe of the ephod" (Ex 29:5) was next. This is the first time the word "robe" is used in the Bible. In the other places it refers to a robe worn by kings and princes. But this was a garment of special dignity which gave a princely character to the office of the priest. No wonder we are spoken of as "a royal priesthood" (1 Pe 2:9).

Nothing is said of the materials from which it was made; we only know that it was blue (Ex 28:31), which speaks of the heavenly calling of the priesthood. The man who knows his calling is from above will not "entangleth himself with the affairs of this life" (2 Ti 2:4). He will not be so heavenly minded that he is no earthly good. This will simply make his calling so noble and great that, like Moses, who "refused to be called the son of Pharaoh's daughter," he will choose "rather to suffer affliction with the people of God, than to enjoy the pleasures of sin for a season; esteeming the reproach of Christ greater riches than the treasures in Egypt; for he had respect unto the recompense of the reward" (Heb 11:24-26).

This robe had a hole at its top, and the hole had a binding of woven work so that it would not be torn (Ex 28:32). On the robe's hem were "pomegranates of blue, and of purple, and of scarlet, round about the hem thereof; and bells of gold between them round about" (28:33). The pomegranate is specially connected with the Holy Land. Pomegranates were brought out by the spies (Num 13:23) as evidence of the fruitfulness of the land. They were not the fruit of Egypt, the picture of the world. The "fruits" there were melons, cucumbers, leeks, onions, and garlic, all of which are grown close to the ground. The pomegranates were always the picture and reminder of fruitfulness. God expects every creature to be fruitful. When the Lord Jesus found the fig tree with leaves only and no fruit, He cursed it. He said to His disciples, "Ye have not chosen me, but I have chosen you, and ordained you, that ye should go and bring forth fruit, and that your fruit should remain" (Jn 15:16). To be consistent, this fruit must include the fruit of the Spirit: love, joy, peace (Gal 5:22), and the fruit of souls (Ro 1:13).

Bells were on the hem of the robe also. "And his sound shall be heard when he goeth in unto the holy place before the LORD, and when he cometh out, that he die not" (Ex 28:35). Nothing else is said about these bells. Much conjecture has been made as to their purpose and meaning. One thing seems obvious; the priests were to keep moving. They could not sit nor stand still. When the nobleman gave the pounds to his servants, he said unto them, "Occupy till I come" (Lk 19:13). The servant who did not put the pound to use but hid it was called a "wicked servant" and was slain (vv. 22-27).

The next piece of the clothing was the ephod itself. As described in Exodus 28:6-14, it was a short outer garment. The ephod was made of two pieces, a front and back joined by two shoulder pieces and by a band around the bottom. On the shoulder straps were two onyx stones set in gold and engraved with the names of the twelve tribes of Israel. "And Aaron shall bear their names before the LORD upon his two shoulders for a memorial" (v. 12b). This was a unique garment, for the fine linen had fine strips of pure gold like wire woven into the linen (39:3). A "curious girdle" or belt made of the same material bound the ephod to the priest (vv. 4-5).

Throughout Scripture "shoulders" represent strength. The names of the children of Israel were borne upon the high priest's shoulders. Moses and Aaron certainly bore the children of Israel up on their journey. Had it not been for Moses' intercession in Exodus 32:30-32, God would surely have destroyed them. Perhaps few churches or Christians realize how often a pastor has intervened for a church before God. Paul spoke of the care of the churches that was upon him (2 Co 11:28). No wonder God's servants are admonished to "be strong and of a good courage" (Jos 1:6; cf. 2 Ti 2:1). The ministry is not a place for the weak and fainthearted, as can be attested by the long list of casualties along the road. The tragic caricature made by Hollywood and TV of a minister being a prissified, effeminate man, sipping tea with old ladies, is almost sacrilegious. Or the weakling given over to the passions of the flesh. No, the minster is a soldier who enters into a battle with the forces of Satan and sin and needs God's divine power woven into his life, as represented by the gold wire.

The breastplate

Perhaps the most beautiful and colorful part of the priest's outfit was the breastplate, as described in Exodus 28:15-29. This was a bib one span (nine inches) square, made of the colorful linen entwined with gold wire as in the ephod (vv. 14-16). It was doubled to form a pouch in which were placed the mysterious Urim and Thummim (v. 30). Set in the breastplate were four rows of precious stones, three in each row and each stone engraved with the name of one of the children of Israel. This breastplate hung by chains of gold from the shoulder pieces of the ephod. One of the most solemn and beautiful statements of God's Word is said about this breastplate and its place in the ministry:

> And Aaron shall bear the names of the children of Israel in the breastplate of judgment upon his heart, when he goeth in unto the holy place, for a memorial before the LORD continually. And thou shalt put in the breastplate of judgment the Urim and the Thummim; and they shall be upon Aaron's heart, when he goeth in before the LORD: and Aaron shall bear the judgment of the children of Israel upon his heart before the LORD continually.

As absolutely strange as it may seem, nothing is said about the Urim and Thummim to let us know just what they were or how they were used. The meaning of the words is accepted by many to be "lights and perfections." Much speculation has been made as to how they were used. Josephus and other early writers have given no precise information about them. In some way these were used to find God's will. God said Joshua "shall stand before Eleazar the priest, who shall ask counsel for him after the judgment of Urim before the LORD; at his word shall they go out, and at his word they shall come in" (Num 27:21). The discerning of God's will for the people and the directing of them in the way He desired were serious and awesome tasks, but the priest was equipped to do them. No wonder God speaks of those who have the rule over His people today (Heb 13:7, 17). The people are to follow God's appointed leaders; all sheep need a shepherd. God's shepherds must seek counsel from God and be ready to answer in eternity for each decision. A pastor is fully equipped with the Holy Spirit indwelling him to lead him.

The rest of the breastplate provided the controls to correct leadership. Aaron was to "bear the names of the children of Israel . . . upon his heart . . . before the LORD continually" (Ex 28:29). This surely suggests a love for the people and also assures that they would be held up before the Lord. When

God's people are on a pastor's heart like that, they will listen to his preaching and follow his leading. Most people in churches are starved to death for a pastor's love. If he loves them and they know it, he can preach as hard and straight as he wants and they will not be offended. The people must be on his heart to do this; then they must be borne before the Lord continually.

Instruction is then given to "gird him with the curious [beautifully woven] girdle of the ephod" (29:5). This was not a girdle in today's ordinary sense of the word. It was simply a beautifully woven belt to bind the breastplate to the priest. Daily the priest went in before the Lord at the altar of incense but always with the people on his heart. A pastor's ministry will be sweeter and more successful if his people are continually bound to his heart.

The miter

"And thou shalt put the mitre upon his head, and put the holy crown upon the mitre" (29:6). "Miter" comes from a Hebrew word meaning "to roll or wind around." This was not the miter worn today by Roman Catholic priests, but, rather, it is like a turban or a tiara. On a golden plate fastened to this miter was engraved "HOLINESS TO THE LORD" (39:30-31). It is called "the holy crown" in Exodus 29:6.

The practice of covering the head reveals a great and glorious truth. In 2 Samuel 15, "Absalom stole the hearts of the men of Israel" (v. 6). Absalom, in an act of treason, rebelled and declared that he would reign over the people of God at Hebron. David heard about it in Jerusalem and fled for fear. David then sought to know what God would have him do. The Ark of God was carried into Jerusalem "and David went up by the ascent of mount Olivet, and wept as he went up, and had his head covered, and he went barefoot: and all the people that was with him covered every man his head, and they went up, weeping as they went up" (v. 30). Jeremiah 14:3 says, "They were ashamed and confounded, and covered their heads." From these and other references, this head covering was a sign of humility and submission, summed up in the New Testament: "Humble yourselves therefore under the mighty hand of God, that he may exalt you in due time" (1 Pe 5:6). There was such a reverence of God by the priests that they humbled themselves and showed their submission by covering their heads. David went up barefoot, suggesting that he felt he was coming before God on holy ground.

To be used of God today, God's servants need a heartfelt humility before God at even the thought of being His servants. Often in the Old Testament, kings and others tore their clothes and poured ashes on their heads as a sign of humility before God. Today men of God often feel like doing the same and, with broken and contrite hearts, fall on their faces and in their hearts prostrate themselves in like manner before God. No matter how great the preachers or the ministry, men must be "little in thine own sight" (1 Sa 15:17). Crowned with this diadem, a pastor will see his influence for God spread far and wide. God hates a haughty and arrogant spirit. No man will see mighty exploits for God without submission to God.

The golden plate with "HOLINESS TO THE LORD" (Ex 28:36) before the priest and upon him must have reminded him of God's demand, "Ye shall be holy; for I am holy" (Lev 11:44). God's servants must be crowned with holiness. No matter how the term has been misused, men are to "worship the LORD in the beauty of holiness" (Ps 29:2).

The Consecration of the Priests

After the priests were called and clothed, they were to be consecrated: "And thou shalt speak unto all that are wise hearted, whom I have filled with the spirit of wisdom, that they may make Aaron's garments to consecrate him, that he may minister unto me in the priest's office (Ex 28:3). The Hebrew word qodesh means "set apart." It is often translated "sanctify." Most people have a set of dishes that are sanctified, set apart from everyday use to be used only when guests come or on special occasions. The priests were set apart from the chores and labor in order to be used only in

119

this service for God. Today we "ordain" men to the Gospel ministry. This does not make them more holy than others. They should be set apart because, as Aaron, they are called by God to this ministry. As Aaron, symbolically they should be clothed with "holy garments" before consecration!

Gathering before the people

Leviticus 8 gives details of this consecration. First, it was done in the sight of all the people. "And gather thou all the congregation together unto the door of the tabernacle of the congregation" (v. 3). Nothing was done in secret. No mysterious or hidden rites were performed. None dared gather just a few intimate friends or followers and declare themselves priests. How often throughout history has this been done, and invariably some cult or schism has begun. God just doesn't work that way. The tragedy is that some foolishly follow such leaders, and more wrecks are wrought.

Washing of the priests

Then "Moses brought Aaron and his sons, and washed them with water" (v. 6). The washing with water, as was seen in the laver, is cleansing from daily defilement. It is the application of 1 John 1:9. Now the Lord Jesus, who washes us from our daily defilement, is the One corresponding to Moses. Our Christian life is a walk, and when we sin after salvation we get our feet dirty. When Peter protested Christ washing his feet, Jesus said, "If I wash thee not, thou hast no part with me" (Jn 13:8). As noted before, the meaning is "You will not participate with me in what I am doing." For the priests to be used of God, they needed cleansing from daily dirt.

Recently I saw a stewardess on a plane lose her patience with a passenger and act rather rudely. She was boiling with anger for most of the trip. Just before landing, although she was not solely at fault, the stewardess came and apologized to the passenger. She humbled herself but exalted herself in my eyes. Sometimes Christians don't apologize when they are in the wrong. Many seldom confess specific sins to the Lord; but, to be used of God, His servants must!

Clothing the priests

Then the priests were clothed with the garments of beauty and glory. First, Aaron, the high priest, was anointed with oil. This was done before the sacrifices were slain and the blood applied (Lev 8:12). Here Aaron stands uniquely representing Christ our High Priest, as the sinless One with no need of the application of the blood. It was said of the Lord Jesus, "God giveth not the Spirit by measure unto him" (Jn 3:34). And again of Him it was said, "Thy God, hath anointed thee with the oil of gladness above thy fellows" (Heb 1:9).

Applying the blood

Now comes a very solemn and sacred moment (Lev 8:14-26). The bullock was sacrificed and the blood applied. First the blood was sprinkled on and poured out at the altar. This was done once and for all by the Lord Jesus at Calvary, and salvation is assured once and for all. Then Moses brought the ram for consecration (v. 22). Aaron and his sons laid their hands on the head of the ram, claiming this one for themselves as their own sacrifice (v. 22). "And he slew it; and Moses took of the blood of it, and put it upon the tip of Aaron's right ear, and upon the thumb of his right hand, and upon the great toe of his right foot" (v. 23). This personal application of the blood was to be on the ear for what he heard, on the hand for what he did, and on the toe for where he went. Every part of God's servant's ministry needs the blood applied. Thus they became very personally identified with the sacrifice and its death.

There must be a very personal identification of God's servants today with the death of Christ, not only for salvation but for service, for "except a corn of wheat fall into the ground and die, it abideth alone: but if it die, it bringeth forth much fruit" (Jn 12:24). Yes, a man must die to sin and self or he abides alone. The praise and pomp must not inflate him, nor the suffering and shame deflate him. He must from the depth of his soul say, "I am crucified with Christ" (Gal 2:20).

What a beautiful picture was enacted by the priest at this point. The Scriptures declare, "And he put all upon Aaron's hands, and upon his son's hands, and waved them for a wave offering before the LORD" (Lev 8:27). The priest's hands were filled with parts of the ram and the unleavened cakes. This was then waved to and fro in the air before the Lord. Now "Moses took the breast, and waved it for a wave offering before the LORD" (v. 29). Whatever else its meaning is, it appears that as the priest laid his hand on the sacrifice, identifying himself with the sacrifice, he now makes a presentation of the sacrifice to God by waving it before the Lord. In doing this he is presenting himself to the Lord.

Anointing with the oil

Now comes that great and glad anointing of the priests with "oil" (v. 30). This oil was sacred and sweet (Ex 30:31). To try to duplicate it meant death (v. 33).

Too many are trying to duplicate the anointing of the Holy Spirit in many different unscriptural ways. No wonder their efforts cause division and dissension and often lead to ultimate defeat and disillusionment, as witnessed in much of the modern-day emphasis on the Holy Spirit and gifts of the Holy Spirit in erroneous ways.

Notice it was not to put "upon a stranger" (v. 33). "If any man have not the Spirit of Christ, he is none of his" (Ro 8:9). God definitely does not give the Holy Spirit to anyone but to those who have received Jesus Christ as their own personal Saviour. Too many are trying to claim some "anointing of the Holy Spirit" today without an ounce of knowledge of being born again. This should not be so.

The climax, which was the consecration, comes as God says, "And thou shalt anoint Aaron and his sons, and consecrate them, that they may minister unto me in the priest's office. And thou shalt speak unto the children of Israel, saying, This shall be an holy anointing oil unto me throughout your generations" (Ex 30:30-31). The priests were now fully supplied and separated to the ministry of God.

There is a parallel to this today. No one can undertake God's work without that conscious, constant dependence on the Holy Spirit of God. Many over the ages have come to a moment of truth at which time they came to a definite decision, deep dedication, and deliberate dependence on the Holy Spirit to work through them. It may have been very climactic, as was Wesley's or Finney's.

It may have been an experience as Moody's, who felt like liquid love was poured out upon him. It may grow into a moment-by-moment realization and yieldedness to the Holy Spirit and be seen only in God's unusual power working through God's preacher; but without that evidence of the Holy Spirit's power, a ministry is barren and a burden.

Christ, quoting Isaiah 61:1-2, said, "The Spirit of the Lord is upon me, because he hath anointed me to preach the gospel to the poor; he hath sent me to heal the brokenhearted, to preach deliverance to the captives, and recovering of sight to the blind, to set at liberty them that are bruised" (Lk 4:18). God's people, and especially His preachers, must have this conscious conviction of the Holy Spirit upon their ministry. A man's ministry will be wanting and wasted without it. The Lord Jesus exhorted His disciples, "And, behold, I send the promise of my Father upon you: but tarry ye in the city of Jerusalem, until ye be endued with power from on high" (Lk 24:49).

Without the Holy Spirit and His presence and power in their ministry, they were powerless. The very last words of the Son of God on this earth were, "Ye shall receive power, after that the Holy Ghost is come upon you: and ye shall be witnesses unto me" (Ac 1:8). Every Christian possesses the Holy Spirit today, but the Holy Spirit does not possess every Christian! It is one thing to have the Holy Spirit; it is quite another for the Holy Spirit to have you, lock, stock, and barrel.

So many are becoming conscious of demon possession.

Often someone is seen with a weird, wild-eyed look of being possessed. It is awesome to see such. What we need, what we must have, are preachers who are just as surely, just as openly, possessed by the Holy Spirit of God! It will not result in a wild, weird, reckless ministry but in a warm, wooing, wonderful ministry in which Christ is preeminent, for "He [the Holy Spirit] shall glorify me [Christ]" (Jn 16:14).

How does this happen? Obviously it is not with the ordination by the hands of men, as can be attested by multitudes of ordained men who are powerless and defeated. John 7:37-39 gives some real clues:

> In the last day, that great day of the feast, Jesus stood and cried, saying, If any man thirst, let him come unto me, and drink. He that believeth on me, as the scripture hath said, out of his belly shall flow rivers of living water. (But this spake he of the Spirit, which they that believe on him should receive: for the Holy Ghost was not yet given; because that Jesus was not yet glorified.)

First comes a thirst: "If any man thirst." A thousand things, such as fame, fortune, fun, friends, or the flesh, can kill God's servants' thirst. It is a catastrophe that it can too often be said today that "there is none that stirreth up himself to take hold of thee" (Is 64:7). Preacher, has that thirst long since been quenched until your heart no longer "pants after God"? Stir yourself; stir up the gift of God in you!

Then "let him come unto me" (Jn 7:37). This may take some "tarrying." Get alone with God. Even a Jacob with all his scheming and failures was transformed into an Israel, a prince with God, when he got alone and wrestled with God. How long has it been since you agonized before God, confessed your sins, covered your head with humility and submission, and cried out to God for a revival in your own heart? Do it now for this fresh anointing, this being possessed by the Holy Spirit.

Then take, "drink," said the Saviour. By faith claim this for yourself. God says, "Understanding what the will of the Lord is . . . be filled with the Spirit" (Eph 5:17-18). Then God, who cannot lie, promised, "If we ask any thing according to his will, . . . we know that we have the petitions we desired" (1 Jn 5:14-15). Will you claim this filling, this control, this being possessed by faith? You tell a lost person to believe God that "whosoever shall call upon the name of the Lord shall be saved" (Ro 10:13). Will you not believe God that "if ye then, being evil, know how to give good gifts unto your children: how much more shall your heavenly Father give the Holy Spirit to them that ask him?" (Lk 11:13). It isn't that we get more of the Holy Spirit, but, in reality, He gets more of us.

Right now, trust and taste, "for out of your innermost belly shall flow rivers of living water . . . this spake he of the Spirit" (Jn 7:38-39). Oh, the joy of seeing a Niagara flowing through you to a dry, dusty drained world. It changes one's ministry from a lonely, powerless labor into a lovely, powerful ministry. To God be the glory, for it will be worth it all when we see Jesus!